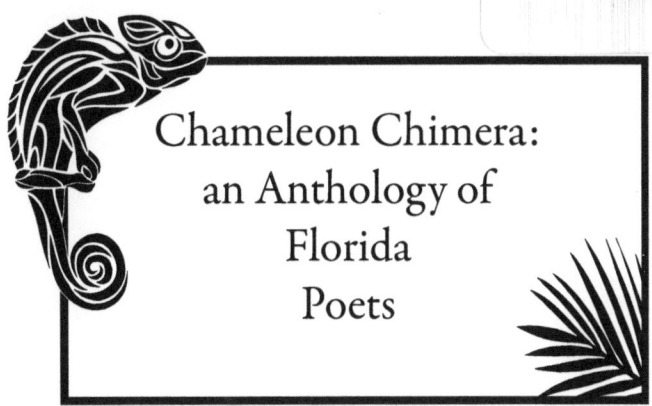

Chameleon Chimera: an Anthology of Florida Poets

Curated
by
Lenny DellaRocca

Editors
Lenny DellaRocca
Yael Valencia Aldana
Madison Whatley

**Purple
Ink Press**

Hollywood,
Florida

Purple Ink Press
5924 Sheridan Street, No. 2128
Hollywood, Florida, 33021
www.purpleinkpress.com

Chameleon Chimera: an Anthology of Florida Poets / edited
by Lenny DelaRocca, Yael Valencia Aldana,
and Madison Whatley. -- 1st ed.
ISBN 979-8-9892793-1-9

Cover by Yael Valencia Aldana
Interior design by Yael Valencia Aldana and Erik Ebright

Cover photograph: Cozy by Zoe Tribley

For all those poets who labor in the dark

THE FLORIDA KEYS

Its own world built on the ocean bed. The ballyhoos bite and dance on board. The Florida keys are awake. The tarpon feed through the winter as the Penta plants spread ashore. The music hears no end here. The loons know the songs. Dive knives glisten. This kiss of earth decorated by lizards and lovers is alive — gulping with fresh gills.

The Florida Keys by Terin Weinberg

Table of Contents

Introduction

When I attended a poetry event at the Delray Beach Library, I had no idea that the idea for this anthology was brewing in the mind of another attendee, Lenny DellaRocca.

Lenny and I were social media friends, but I had not met him in person, and I didn't meet him at this event either. I saw someone I thought was him (It was him) but didn't introduce myself because I wasn't sure.

At the event, prominent local poets shared and read some of their favorite poems. I was there to meet Jubi Arriola-Headley, a fellow poet of Caribbean descent. But it was another poet who inspired Lenny. P. Scott Cunningham read the poem "Elegy and Rant for My Father" by Enid Shomer. It is a raw and beautifully brutal elegy about her problematic and difficult father, far from the expected positivized, sanitized he-would-give-you-the-shirt-off-his-back version that we often find in obituaries and elegies.

Enid Shomer is a Florida poet, and as Lenny sat there listening to her poem, the idea was formed to curate an anthology of Florida poets. Lenny approached this project differently, from a community perspective. Instead of soliciting submissions himself, he approached an initial group of poets and invited them to nominate fellow Florida poets to contribute to the anthology. Each contributor was asked to submit a poem, their neighborhood, and nominate someone else.

Lenny first approached Rita Maria Martinez from Miami, who nominated Mary Block, also from Miami, and Chris Bodor from St. Augustine. The project grew in this way, with poets nominating each other. It snaked its way through Florida, creating a map of poetics and poetic relationships through the state, winding through Miami, Mount Dora, Sebastian, Wilton Manors, Jacksonville, and beyond.

The featured works ebb from Richard Blanco's nostalgic visit to Marco Island, to Julie Marie Wade coming out in the woods as herself, to Gabrielle Aboki's loss of a son and uncle before Sunday, to Maureen Seaton's reveling in the concept of a nemesis.

As you make your way through the book, you will see the featured poet, the poet who nominated them, and where they live in Florida. The book is a chain of poetry from one poet to another and now to you.

I submitted my own poem to the project unaware that the project would eventually land in my hands.

This press, Purple Ink Press, was just forming when Lenny was looking for a publisher for the Florida Anthology. We thought, for our first project, was the anthology too big? Probably yes, but we took a deep breath and dove in. With over 100 poets, this was a huge project for our fledgling press. But how could we resist a project with some of Florida's finest poets? We didn't, and we are so honored to bring this to you as our first project.

Richard's Motel by Michelle K. Robinson

Richard Blanco

neighborhood: Surfside

nominated by (Nicole Tallman)

Looking for The Gulf Motel

There should be nothing here I don't remember . . .

The Gulf Motel with mermaid lampposts
and ship's wheel in the lobby should still be
rising out of the sand like a cake decoration.
My brother and I should still be pretending
we don't know our parents, embarrassing us
as they roll the luggage cart past the front desk
loaded with our scruffy suitcases, two-dozen
loaves of Cuban bread, brown bags bulging
with enough mangos to last the entire week,
our espresso pot, the pressure cooker—and
a pork roast reeking garlic through the lobby.
All because we can't afford to eat out, not even
on vacation, only two hours from our home
in Miami, but far enough away to be thrilled
by whiter sands on the west coast of Florida,
where I should still be for the first time watching
the sun set instead of rise over the ocean.
There should be nothing here I don't remember . . .
My mother should still be in the kitchenette
of The Gulf Motel, her daisy sandals from Kmart
squeaking across the linoleum, still gorgeous
in her teal swimsuit and amber earrings

stirring a pot of arroz-con-pollo, adding sprinkles
of onion powder and dollops of tomato sauce.
My father should still be in a terrycloth jacket

3

smoking, clinking a glass of amber whiskey
in the sunset at the Gulf Motel, watching us
dive into the pool, two boys he'll never see
grow into men who will be proud of him.

There should be nothing here I don't remember . . .

My brother and I should still be playing Parcheesi,
my father should still be alive, slow dancing
with my mother on the sliding-glass balcony
of The Gulf Motel. No music, only the waves
keeping time, a song only their minds hear
ten-thousand nights back to their life in Cuba.
My mother's face should still be resting against
his bare chest like the moon resting on the sea,
the stars should still be turning around them.

There should be nothing here I don't remember . . .

My brother should still be thirteen, sneaking
rum in the bathroom, sculpting naked women
from sand. I should still be eight years old
dazzled by seashells and how many seconds
I hold my breath underwater—but I'm not.
I am thirty-eight, driving up Collier Boulevard,
looking for The Gulf Motel, for everything
that should still be, but isn't. I want to blame
the condos, their shadows for ruining the beach
and my past, I want to chase the snowbirds away
with their tacky mansions and yachts, I want
to turn the golf courses back into mangroves,
I want to find The Gulf Motel exactly as it was
and pretend for a moment, nothing lost is lost.

Anjanette Delgado

neighborhood: Miami

nominated by (Richard Blanco)

My Brother's Girlfriend Worries
(Or, The Mixed Girl's Burden)

Take up the White Man's burden-
Send forth the best ye breed-
Go bind your sons to exile
To serve your captives' need;
To wait in heavy harness,
On fluttered folk and wild-
Your new-caught, sullen peoples,
Half-devil and half-child.

Rudyard Kipling,
Britain's Imperial Poet
"The White Man's Burden," 1899

Stop! He cannot see
this, will never see it,
and if you tell your brother
about it, I'll kill you, I swear,
she says and brings the tweezers close
as if to poke my pupils with the single
bright red pubic hair
she's pulled clean off its follicle
and trapped between metal tips.

Who knows why I back away
from her freak translucent fear?
This terror of being a mix
of white teen freckles over lips
fat and round like plums,
widest of noses, that startled 'fro!
Her fright is foreign to me,
she, open-legged transfixed
by an almost invisible thing.

I'd been jealous, I'll admit.
She, now more his
girlfriend than my friend,
cries, *You don't understand!*
I'm not enough
of anything, not black, not white
a thief,
a poser, no matter what.

And I see then: my brother's jeans
too heavy on this skinny girl who feels
"half-devil, half-child," who worries
what it looks like down there,
thinks she can carry
the weight of man's imperialist hate
in pockets fashioned from her flesh.

Nicole Tallman

neighborhood: Miami

nominated by (Elisa Albo)

Poem for the Soft Boys

Where I come from, there's a season for guns, as if rifles should be celebrated like Christmas.

There's a smell. I'd like to call it November, but it's a special blend of blood, rust, estrus, and a winter so cold it freezes the hair inside my nose.

There's a ritual. It's men dressed in camouflage and hunter orange. It's the law. And they stay out late on the 40 and chug 40s, perch up in trees or shelter in blinds, chew tobacco and build big fires.

Where I come from, it's also about the merchandise. The "Nice Rack" shirts and mounted deer heads on the wall. Not surprisingly, racks are one reason men prize the buck more than the doe.

There's a sound out my window where I come from. It's earsplitting gunfire and the fight between my uncle and cousin who never speak again.

There's a name for the soft boys where I come from, the ones who don't drive big trucks and don't refer to women as broads you just load up and throw in the back.

Where I come from, hunting is a blood sport. And it breeds blood-thirsty boys who think it's ok to say: Do what I say or I'll shoot you.

There's also a mascot: a dead deer, purple gray tongue out, gutted and hanging from the rafters of the garage. The same purple gray of the deer liver my dad left on the counter for my mom to cook.

She said it reminded her of afterbirth and made her gag.

Author's Note: This poem was written in response to the question "Where are you from?"—a question people still ask me in Miami, even though I've been living in South Florida for 18 years. The answer is Michigan. This poem was first published in trampset under the title "Rifle Season," and was republished under the title "Poem for the Soft Boys" in my second book, Poems for the People, and subsequently republished again under the title "Rifle Season" in my third book, *FERSACE*. This poem can't decide which title it likes better.

Night Building by Renzo Del Castillo

Along the Moat Wall, Fort Jefferson, Dry Tortuga by Willy Conley

Elisa Albo

neighborhood: Fort Lauderdale

---

nominated by (Julie Marie Wade)

Volver a Cuba, February 2017

They say you can't go home again, but if you try,
you'll need a taxi driver like Rafael Martín Martín
lounging beside Casa de las Americas in Havana's
El Vedado and smoking a slow cigarette when he
caught me pacing the sidewalk—determined not
to use a legal but rude taxi driver from the stand at
the Hotel Presidente next to my casa particulár--

and offered to drive me to my first home in Miramár.
They say you can't go home, but if you try, you'll
need Rafael willing to drive in circles for an hour,
up and down the other Calle Ocho, entre Septima y
Quinta Avenidas, and finally to park in front of
the garish green three-story building, walk you to
the front door, verify the address, cross the busy

street for a better picture, cross back, stare up from
the sidewalk and help you imagine the wide balconies
not caged in by ugly black metal railings rising to
the ceiling. Is that where your nanny stood with your
year-old self in her arms, wailing to your eighteen-
year-old mami below that the authorities had sealed
the house shut, barred her from entering her own

home after my father had fled the country to avoid

11

imprisonment? Was this where she stood, on this
sidewalk, looking up at one child, another sleeping
inside, her husband at that moment in the sky, their
plans for us to follow uncertain? They say you can't
go. You won't even knock on the door. No one will
come to the window. Mami will glare at pictures

you took with Rafael. She'll study them fifty-five
years after she locked for the last time the door to
her first married apartment and say, No, that's not it.
I don't recognize it. You can't go home. You can
return to the land of your birth when your mother
who carried you out is not keen—to say the least--
on you returning, stepping onto the island you have
never known, the place that scattered her family

forever and buried them on three continents. And
you'll return to the look on her face, the do-what-
ever you-want-I-don't-like-it-and-won't-say-another-
word-about-it face. That one. And, not for the first
time, or the last, she will have been right: Cuba
es bella, llena, basilla, pero no se puede volver.

*Translation: Cuba is beautiful. full, empty, but one can't
go back, ** Thomas Wolfe took the title You Can't Go Home Again
with permission from a conversation with writer Ella Winter
who asked him, "Don't you know you can't go home again?"

Julie Marie Wade

neighborhood: Dania Beach

---

nominated by (Denise Duhamel)

Out Here
For Julie A.

the air is clear the water has gone down under the bridge the same
bridge that once was burning and you've heard the way they say the
daffodils are out now and other kinds of flowers by which they mean
their green stems have given rise to blossoms and you are blooming
too the fist of your heart clenched so tight for so long inside you now
slowly unfurling the air is clear though you may be breathing heavy
your voice a slim missile of light against the vast dark landscape you
wonder who can even hear you out here if anyone is even listening the
stars peer back merely curious tracing your whereabouts as you once
traced theirs the moon has been accused of phases too but marvels how
they still say constant as the moon an orbit is not a weakness a body
heavenly or otherwise is not a metaphor just think of the first time you
ever wandered into the woods someone told you to hide so you ran to-
ward the nearest thicket crouching down counting silently to yourself
in the underbrush fearing at first the rustle of feet but later fearing the
absence of the rustle had they forgotten you after all out of sight out of
mind? the air was thick with smoke someone had been burning leaves
it was late autumn and you followed the spice of the wind toward a
clearing you had never felt so small as when you stood in the center of
the open field but your lungs swelled you shouted and heard the out in
it even then the way your throat became a bright flower a tulip huge
and red opening in the unobstructed light of the wrong season olly
olly oxen free! it was a forecast but you didn't know that then a rally-
ing cry you wanted them to find you so much the daylight broad the
future faraway as the riverhead or the ending of a fairy tale and when
at last they came they were waving with their mittens on fingers fused
into a single woolen spade you followed when they said there was a fire

a wild fire they said and even then you wondered if there was any other kind tonight the air is clear the spring indisputable as dew the crisp cool newness of it which is sometimes called splendor and sometimes called terror you raise your hand like a flare you close your eyes and stutter come out come out wherever you are! you are waiting under the new moon beneath the loom of these impossible trees but we are coming I promise we are rustling our way toward you murmuring welcome! some of us rain-swept some of us wind-shook though some of us are closer than you can imagine some of us are glowing like fireflies our small light unmistakable some of us are already here

Originally published in *New Letters*

Pink Sky by Sharon L. Green

15

Denise Duhamel

neighborhood: Hollywood

---

nominated by (Gregg Shapiro)

FORTUNATELY, UNFORTUNATELY, FLORIDA

Fortunately, I live by the sea.
Unfortunately, the sea is dying.
Fortunately, for me, the blob of seaweed is on the west coast.
Unfortunately, the east coast of Florida where I live has sharks.
Fortunately, the sharks prefer to eat other fish.
Unfortunately, overfishing has wiped out a lot of shark meals.
Fortunately, lifeguards keep watch from 10-6.
Unfortunately, those lifeguards are often distracted, on their phones.
Fortunately, phones provide charts about jellyfish blooms.
Unfortunately, a jellyfish can float away from the others.
Fortunately, pink moon jellies are easy for humans to spot.
Unfortunately, clear comb jellyfish are sometimes undetectable.
Fortunately, most jellyfish stings cause pain and swelling, but that's
    about it.
Unfortunately, the sting of certain box jellies (or sea wasps) are fatal.
Fortunately, the pain of most stings can be relieved with vinegar.
Unfortunately, some people think human urine will help.
Fortunately, this myth makes for some good jokes.
Unfortunately, some of those jokes will be banned if our governor
    has anything to say about it.
Fortunately, some banned books gain a wider readership.
Unfortunately, the governor wants to ban AP Black history courses.
Fortunately, students are making impromptu study groups, teaching
    themselves.

Unfortunately, impromptu study groups are not available to everyone.
Fortunately, abortion is still available in some states.
Unfortunately, abortion is restricted to six weeks in Florida.

Fortunately, I kept my "Keep Abortion Save and Legal" bumper
sticker from the 70s.
Unfortunately, that bumper sticker is relevant again.
Fortunately, I still feel relevant when I write about these things.
Unfortunately, I sometimes feel scared to write what I feel.
Fortunately, I'm still feeling something.
Unfortunately, I feel rage and fear because of the mass shooting on
      Hollywood Beach.
Fortunately—well, there aren't many fortunate things to say
      about guns.
Unfortunately, I'm feeling outnumbered by bigots.
Fortunately, my rational brain knows there are more of my kind
      than theirs.
Unfortunately, more drag queens and LGBTQ+ folk are under attack.
Fortunately, they have senses of humor—*Rhonda DeSatan,*
      keep drag queens safe from children!
Unfortunately, Ron isn't gracious when it comes to laughing
      at himself.
Fortunately, Ron's rigid thinking would make him lose at improv.
Unfortunately, over 2000 sea creatures are threatened
      according to the Endangered Species Act.
Fortunately, it's sunny today with wild waves—and I am a creature
      who loves the sea.

Untitled Colonialtown Orlando 1 by Ryan Rivas

Maureen Seaton

neighborhood: Miami

---

nominated by (Denise Duhamel)

Sweet World

I never had a nemesis before. I kinda like it.

Wonder what I'd be today if I was still married to my Wall Street husband
besides married to a Wall Street husband and puking gin in a silk sheath

at Delmonico's. I might be a blond size 4. I might be a secret Democrat
or a weekend lesbian. This morning five planes flew over the yard in a V

as I was about to dig into a pile of lavender pancakes al fresco. The V
flew low and slow. It flew loud and ominous. It alarmed me, sounding

a lot like the war movies of my fifties' childhood. My cranky Chihuahua
was proverbially biting at flies and I was sitting there not thinking about hate.

Recently, I experienced life with cancer. An intoxicating time, richly infused
with the liquor of death, but good too because no one expected much of me

and I was left to my own mind, which is what I'm missing most these days.
Unless that's it over there, screeching on two wheels around the racetrack.

Today I typed gnos instead of song and I wondered if it was some new app
designed to mess with me. I've never thought to call the world sweet before.

A nemesis can do that for you, make things taste different. Suddenly you're
a hero/ine. All this devastation—and you're still standing in the middle of it.

Originally published in Maureen's book *Sweet World*

Untitled Colonialtown Orlando 2 by Ryan Rivas

A Tribute to Maureen Seaton

by Julie Marie Wade

I wonder who I'd be today if I had never met Maureen Seaton. Not quite the poet, not quite the collaborator, not quite the person, I'm sure. Maureen was the opposite of a nemesis. She didn't naysay—she yaysayed! Word says this isn't a word, but I disagree, and I know Maureen would, too, my sweet friend, sweet neologist.

There was nothing in the world like having Maureen Seaton believe in you, and her belief in all of us, our shared humanity, was capacious, enormous. She didn't give up on people. She helped them expand their possibilities by being such an elastic person, always open, even to the impossible. I loved her before I knew her, through her poems. I loved her after I knew her, beyond them. When I graduated from high school in 1997, there was probably no poet I needed to read more than Maureen Seaton or Denise Duhamel or their collaborations. I was lonely then, doubting that anyone would want to collaborate with me in life, let alone art. I wish I had known there were living poets out there, collaborative poets, too, whose talent and generosity were coming to buoy me into my future life.

For graduation, my Aunt Linda, who dabbled in poetry but was always shy about it, gave me a cookie jar in the likeness of a yellow Volkswagen bug cookie jar. "I know this is your dream car," she said, "and while I can't give you the car to take to college, here's something you can take." I kept special mementos in that cookie jar along with plenty of notecards for jotting down ideas, snippets from poems I loved, and snippets of poems I was going to write. The cookie jar-qua-keepsake mobile still sits on the desk in my office, full to brimming, its contents pushing the top upward, ever more precarious.

Imagine when Maureen Seaton published The Cave of the Yellow Volkswagen in 2009. I reveled in the auspicion of it, by then a long-time fan. Imagine when I moved to Florida in 2012 and became her neighbor, became her friend—the auspicion of that, the sweetness. When Maureen experienced life with cancer and moved out west to Colorado, we kept in touch, of course. I hated to think of her no longer making her annual road trip from Miami to Longmont each summer, then back again in the fall, so I went on eBay and found the identical yellow Volkswagen bug cookie jar that my aunt had given to me and sent it to her. When we Zoomed, I saw it there, always in the frame.

Thank goodness Maureen wasn't shy about her poetry. Thank goodness she kept sharing it right until the end of her life. She was never a poet who spun wheels but a poet who threw her life into drive and floored us all, "gaily forward." Always gaily forward. I'm sure she would have liked that phrase, thrown her head back, and guffawed the way she did.

As a Lutheran only child who was sent to Catholic school, I thought I had become fluent in all the Catholic rituals. But there was one that always eluded me: praying to the saints. I didn't have a special saint to wear on a necklace or a second name given to me during baptism that drew me closer to one of those transcendent human beings, favored and blessed by God. I never prayed to anyone but God during my long school days, and even my prayers were shaky, uncertain. My better prayers were poems. They always have been.

But now, in light of Maureen's passing from this world, I wonder if perhaps she was my special saint all along—secular but no less transcendent for it--someone raised Catholic, someone with a rich spirituality that couldn't be contained by any religious tradition, someone who invited emulation and embodied generosity of spirit. Maureen didn't judge; she inspired, relentlessly.

These days, I find myself talking to Maureen, maybe like a prayer, but less shaky, more certain. I could never be agnostic about Maureen Seaton. Where her life and work are concerned, I will always be a true believer. "Hey, Maureen," I say in the car—no need for Bluetooth to find a connection. "Hey, Maureen," I say as I jog past her one-time bungalow on Hollywood Beach. She's everywhere, ubiquitous as the South Florida sun and the South Florida storms. "How are you?" I say, revving the engine of my heart, summoning her before I teach a class or write a poem: my sweet friend, sweet intercessor.

Holly Iglesias

nominated by (Maureen Seaton)

KANNAPOLIS, 1941, REEL 2
—*after Movies of Local People* by H. Lee Waters

So beautiful the men in hats, the straw boaters, and fedoras, and caps.
So beautiful the ladies in ladies' dresses, summer cottons, dotted Swiss,
      gingham checks, rowdy plaids.
So beautiful the string bag of onions and the basket of canned goods and
      the boxes tied with twine.
So beautiful the children holding hands, bashful in front of the camera,
      two of them toothless.
So beautiful the youth leaving the mill, overalls flecked with thread,
sleeves rolled up to show off his muscles, machine oil on his
      chin.
So beautiful the girl, whippet-thin and haughty, rushing to move past the
Camera until someone shouts her name and she breaks into a
      smile.
So beautiful the men smoking on the curb outside the courthouse, the
      lawyer strolling behind them in a seersucker suit and two-tone
      shoes.
So beautiful the mule pulling a wagon heaped with cartons of peaches and
      berries, so beautiful the driver of the wagon and the mule.
So beautiful the grocer in a pristine apron, unrolling the awnings to protect
      the lettuce from the noonday sun.
So beautiful the grandma in her housedress and lace-up shoes, a boy on one
      hand, a girl on the other, each licking a lollipop.
So beautiful the bodies passing by, so beautiful the haircuts and cloth
      jackets, so beautiful the dungarees spiffed up with a Sunday shirt.
So beautiful the plate of navy beans with ham and red-eye gravy and two
      yeast rolls to sop up the gravy.
So beautiful the girls who scowl, the girls who grin, so beautiful the boy
      who looks away.

So beautiful the mothers outside the shoe store, gazing at the new pumps
    and oxfords behind the glass.
So beautiful the running board where the men rest, chewing the fat,
    bone-tired and laughing.
So beautiful the tongues licking ice cream cones, so beautiful the bare arms
    and sun-suits, so beautiful the hats set at flirtatious angles.
So beautiful the man behind the lens, the man who loves their flowing by,
    so beautiful the river of their days.

Steve Kronen

neighborhood: Miami

---

nominated by (Holly Iglesias)

Schrödinger's Cab

They did not dare take a taxi to the station for fear their departure might
be reported to the authorities.

> Schrödinger: Life and Thought —Walter J. Moore

You won't be sure of its arrival
until it rolls up to your curb.
Wave, the cabbie'll say, *farewell.*

All you own's inside your satchel.
The cabbie says you'll beat the curfew —
you won't be sure if he's a rival,

or if these roads lead to the terminal
where, huddled in their roundhouse, cars
points to or from the far walls

of your city. You'll pat your pockets for the schedule.
The cab backfires and hugs its curve
and you won't be sure if it's a rifle

or why the heart, beating out the spatial,
is agitated at its core,
something at the center feral:
these posted signs, the engine's purr, your travel-
ing light along this course.
You won't be sure just how your eye falls
where you're bound, or why that feels, in passing, like free will.

from *The New Statesman*

Peter Schmitt

neighborhood: Miami

nominated by (Steve Kronen)

Friends with Numbers

If you make friends with numbers, you don't need any other friends.
    —Shakuntala Devi, math genius

They are not hard to get to know:
6 and 9 keep changing their minds,
8 cuts the most graceful figure
but sleeps for an eternity,
and 7, lucky 7, takes
an arrow to his heart always.
5, halfway to somewhere, only
wants to patch his unicycle
tire, and 4, who'd like to stand for
something solid, has never had
two feet on the ground, yet flutters
gamely in the breeze like a flag.
3, for all his literary
accomplishments and pretensions
to immortality, is still
(I can tell you) not half the man
8 is asleep or awake. 1,
little 1. I know him better
than all the others, these numbers
who are all my friends. Only 2,
that strange smallest prime, can I count
as just a passing acquaintance.
Divisible by only 1
and herself, she seems on the verge,
yet, of always coming apart.
And though she eludes me, swanlike,
though I'd love to know her better,
still I am fine, there are others,
many, I have friends in numbers.

Originally published in *Hazard Duty* (Copper Beech Press, 1995)

Avocado Ave by Renzo Del Castillo

Gregg Shapiro

neighborhood: Fort Lauderdale

nominated by (Lenny DellaRocca)

Polly Amorous

Can you hear the parrots of Manor Grove
over the traffic on Andrews Avenue?
They are arguing or laughing. They are
gossiping or singing, rehearsing choral
numbers and solos for a concert. Clannish
and bossy. Possessive and demanding.
Issuing directives about predatory hawks.
They fear no squirrel, raccoon or iguana.

Can you find them on the branches blending
in with leaves the color of their feathers?
You rarely see them on the ground, waddling
through the duck-trodden grass. Avoiding
the yellow bamboo stalks where they stand
out like Pentecostals at a porn shoot. Flying
in cacophonous formation, waiting for someone
to notice, perhaps write a poem about them.

Originally published in *Panoplyzine*

Untitled Colonialtown Orlando 4 by Ryan Rivas

Dustin Brookshire

neighborhood: Wilton Manors

nominated by (Gregg Shapiro)

Revisionist Villanelle

Columbus couldn't navigate for shit,
but that isn't how his story is told.
There is too much history we don't admit.

If you praise Columbus— quit.
He chopped off hands for lack of gold.
The man couldn't navigate for shit.

In 1500, Ferdinand found Columbus unfit.
Spaniards were tired of being controlled.
There is too much history we don't admit.

Columbus was stripped of his governorship,
but still funded to find more gold,
even though he couldn't navigate for shit.

A tyrant, murderer, enslaver. A culprit
textbooks let get away. So many sins untold.
There is too much history we don't admit:

Columbus was a sex trafficker. We omit,
and no one knows how many girls he sold.
Christopher Columbus is a piece of shit.
There is too much history we don't admit.

Originally published in *Oddball Magazine*

Yuki Jackson

neighborhood: Tampa

---

nominated by (Dustin Brookshire)

Katara (for real)

I am the One
who brought the great flood
of warriors onto your shore–
roaring, majestic life from the Motherland,
hear that rumble–
our gale force winds have broke the chains,
see it all come rushing as change–
so fast best believe that's whiplash
on behalf of the ancestors–
in fact we are them–

you see the energy stored
from all the injustice we bore
only passed on–
isn't bending blood
just like bending water?
the avatar of God, call me Katara

truth is, we began at the bottom–
in that space so dark and deep,
we couldn't be seen–
the only light is produced from our own heads,
projected in third eye position–

it is here where pressure is most profound,
where we make our way through the rhythm of sound,
manifesting waves from our vibration–
this is what it means to sea deeply,
that bass throbbing as pulse that begins tsunami–

born from the underground,
that place closest to the core,
creating waves as crescendo,
following lines that lead us to the peak
above that mountain in the distance–

you know energy travels as spirals,
winding up like a cork to pop the top off this bottle,
shaken up, this blood we drink to form our sanctity–
isn't it once there was no word for the color blue,
so we called the sea "blood"–
like the stream we laid the beat upon,
with enough room to lay our verses
and move the masses
even before we perform–

this means the mass we gained
has been invisible–
but it's been stacking up,
all this pressure,
all this attempt to hold us down
has only made us stronger–

no we are not woke,
we are awake,
as in a wake,
as in those ocean waves created
when a vessel moves through a medium,
as in the medium cannot be compressed,
as in this wake cannot be suppressed,
as in the wake when we gather
to pay respects to the dead with their body present–
I am that body who gave all this labor–
"what life through yonder water breaks?"

this is the real Genesis,

meaning these are the generations,
a generator cord pumping through these children,
aka warriors,
best believe these MC's came out by the dozen–
you can't fade the mother of all creation,
the original, the source,
follow me and you'll find your birth–
to return to that side we lost,
making us complete
in this narrative of human history–

we are the evolution,
the new branch in the story–
but in order to understand life,
you must reckon with your birth–

even Hokusai couldn't imagine
what was coming–

born as arsenal to seal our fate,
best believe I came to slay–
and here I will deliver the arc–
not as in a ship to escape,
as in we ARE the great flood–
like the arc in my arm raised
as they bow to my power–

I am the Great Wave Off Kanagawa,
I'm atomic, I'm nuclear–
and now we're in the delivery room–
you wanna know how the universe began?
One word: BOOM

Originally published in *Creative Loafing Tampa Bay*

Old brace by Sean E. Sexton

Jessica Q. Stark

neighborhood: Jacksonville

---

nominated by (Dustin Brookshire)

In Want of a Quiet Place
    for Cora

The news is featureless today, which feels oceanic—a calm, threatening place
marker between catastrophes. Tomorrow, there will be more tongues on the
vacated state of some anonymous womb, some new language for
rubbernecking desire, some paralyzing provision on more men holding guns
holding hostages holding guns in this haughty age of deep-sea, sedating rage.

Most powerful women scandal-suck marrow and then find a new
name, so let me state her plain: Cora Ethel Eaton Howarth, Cora Murphy,
Cora Stewart with a shake-less chaperone, Cora Cora Cora Crane making
coffee, Cora Taylor, Hotel of Dreams.

And my favorite: Imogene Carter—savvy-saw war correspondent vying for a
novelmind and another nation on behalf of women, though she admits out
there she only found more men plucking flowers for dead stones.

Every neighbor she met was a thesaurus for *bad woman* on the basis of
 too much or too little love. Every storm scale is a matter of perspective. At
the turn of the century, a red light provided both theater and information:
copaiba oil for stomach cancer. Mercury, arsenic, and vinegar for a different
face.

Once, I was determined to re-read the review that underscores my
ambition, and with that, I was enlisted. Danced it near-naked for student
loan forgiveness--to forgive me. Or the time I was tipped a phone number
at Duke's Bar in Midtown and smiled at the candid tedium of my feminine
situation. Look, this poem has a seam, too, and I'm in it for the gamble.
I'm in it for the *information*, for the pursuit and rise of whole buildings of
women moving breathlessly next door.

But mostly, I'm in want of some quiet place, Cora Cora, aren't you?
Some footpath out of this invisible battlefield. It takes so much
thinking to make a life, to make a decent dress. It takes so much
of me to resist horizontal living.

A contemporary review of Cora's failed writing stresses that her stories
graze a purpose, but they never come to full fruition—all rumination, no
point, not enough blast. Cora's grave features the wrong birthdate. Her
death date, too.

There's no fabric to a pointing limb, but the reviewer did include an
accurate description of the cause of death.

She died on the beach after trying to move a car that was trapped—stone
stuck--to way down deep in the sand.

Dorsey Craft

neighborhood: Jacksonville

---

nominated by (Jessica Q Stark)

Rejected Persona: Influencer

Bury me in pearly packaging—glass
bottles, sage green, buff peach. *This is
the Dior in shade MG4. This is the Glam
Shine Glow Glitz Fairy Cootchie in shade NC7.*

Where to go from here? Maybe pivot
to mommy content—Do Moses baskets
come with warnings? NOT a flotation device.
NOT an allusion, metaphor, or simile.

There is only so much space in the cloud
for my ass in mom jeans, tilt hips, pop knee,
skinny arm, lose the possessive "my," lose
the feminine "her". I told my mom

I'm playing with my gender and she goes
"I guess I have aways played with mine"
and I was like Yes, bitch, exactly. Get ready with me.
I want to do one side of my face in hibiscus,

the other deer blood. Body fluids are the brand.
So is violence, like do not call me, I am busy
layering serums, snatching my contour,
suggested reel /suggested real. It's clean

because we say it's clean. I litter used language:
daisy-fresh, feather-light, butter-smooth.
I am the active ingredient. I want to live surprise-free,
scroll-dazed, soul washed pink as a millennium.

Untitled Colonialtown Orlando 3 by Ryan Rivas

Tyler Gillespie

neighborhood: St. Petersburg

nominated by (Dustin Brookshire)

britney spears argues a specific worldview. posits

Britney Spears argues a specific worldview. Posits
only two types of people exist: the ones that entertain

& the ones that observe. Other theorists may disagree.

(Judith Butler et al recognize the performed nature
of gender – so who isn't performing? – & we trace

poetry's roots to song, to orality etc. etc. etc.).

Britney's binary might seem reductive, but her framework
proves useful for us to consider the active/passive
nature of existence: the (in)action of choice. Consequence of being.

She asserts it's better to dance (entertain) than to stand (observe).

I'm usually against such absolutism in judgment but if pressed yesterday
I would have agreed. Today, though, I'm not so sure.

Originally published in *mutiny!* as well as Tyler's book *the nature machine!*

Maureen McDole

neighborhood: St. Petersburg

nominated by (Tyler Gillespie)

My Grandmother's Curtains

Pink sheer curtains swelled in the girls'
room when my mother was growing up.
She shared the pink shades with her sisters.
When I spent nights in that room, those curtains'
shadows scared me away from sleep.
A framed felt picture loomed over the hallway
that led to the bathroom: a group of dogs playing poker.
I swear they stared at me until I shut the door.
The walk-in closet was a meeting place for ghosts.
It wasn't safe to sleep with two eyes closed.
As an adult, I claimed the pink curtains
when my grandmother passed and the house sold.
I hung them in my bedroom and learned to love
the color they bred with the light. My once lover
named it Womb Room, a place I reclaimed.

Letisia Cruz

neighborhood: St. Petersburg

---

nominated by (Maureen McDole)

Nothing of Beauty

The summer I was 11
I learned from Yanina and Yvette--
girls much older than I—that the religion
of women who wear lipstick is beauty.
Beauty. I wore no lipstick then,
had no religion. But I could disappear
into any room. Blend into the wallpaper.
At times I wondered--
do I even exist?

One night under a summer diluvio,
I stood outside our green
apartment building
watching the neighbors run
from the bodega to the laundromat,
to the corner bar. The sun sank lower
casting orange shadows on the front steps,
and I faded. Not a single soul lay witness.

The religion I learned as a child
was not beauty, but survival.
I did not know it by name
then. But I knew the sounds--
the timbre and cadence of gunshots.
Hurricanes rushing for shore. Fists
breaking over my mother's face.
Now the stars were all
dim. A Friday night

and I sat in the back seat of Wilma's Buick
parked a block from her boyfriend's house
with the windows rolled up,
the engine turned off.

Wilma and my mother eyed the front door
like little hawks waiting
for someone to swoop in with dinner.
Wilma sank lower behind the wheel,
eyes full of flames.
I'd seen the same look
in my mother's. The man strolled
out the front door and we followed.
Love makes us hungry,
my mother said.

My stomach grumbled.
Hunger, too, was religion. But one
I already knew would fail me.
How hunger, like beauty,
leaves you vulnerable.
Makes you forget where you are--
in a car. In a field.
Under water.
Locked up in the basement
of your own house.
Not survival. My religion
was the worship of place.

This—here and now. This.
Open your eyes. By god girl,
don't you ever forget it.

Religion is a barred window.
The flame of a match. A sky void of stars.
The smell of burnt rice. Fog.

Religion is your mother's long hair.
Burning. Your father's smile.
The way he looked at her.
Then darkness. Nothing but night.
The place you came to as a child.
Your abandoned reservoir.
Your escape. Religion
is setting your crosses on fire.
Holding nothing of beauty.
No hunger.

How the night sky is wide open.

Originally published in *Migrations & Other Exiles*, (Lost Horse Press, 2023)

Sara Ries Dziekonski

neighborhood: St. Petersburg

nominated by (Maureen McDole)

Rewind

The days are not equal mixing bowls
of time. A moment can be a slow stir
through the country, or a dash to another
country, map melted in mouth,
　　　　new set of keys jingling in your pocket.
A glance can be a year, or a walk down
the stairs, like how my closer to three
than four year old came down post nap so
casually, said *Hi Mommy.*

　　　　He used to call my name
　　　　　　when he woke, and I'd rub his back
until he was ready to be lifted from the crib
to rejoin the world.
　　　　We'd rock back
and forth, then peek through the blinds
at the house being built next door.
　　　　I'd hum him a song I used to listen to
when I was small, incessantly pressing rewind
on my CD player to jot down every lyric
of my favorite songs on silver moons.

　　　But today
　　　　　　is a stone skipped into
　　　many tomorrows, and my son 　　got older
in one sleep.

He came down so casually, said *Hi Mommy*
as though about to grab cereal and pour
himself a bowl, / came down
so casually as though swinging
a backpack over his sturdy shoulder to catch
the bus / came down so casually
as though about to fix his coffee
and locate his briefcase, / came down so casually
as though I am on the sofa of   his house,
       and he's about to ask me
   if I've remembered to take my medicine / —

My son came down so casually,
and there's not one unscratched /
    way to rewind.

Terry Godbey

neighborhood: Orlando

nominated by (Susan Lilley)

Finding Love at 66

Maybe there is nothing, ever, that can equal the recollection of having been young together.
—Michael Cunningham

I opened the Facebook message and out came an old friend

I opened the old friend and out came a man who fell for me decades ago

I opened the man who fancied me without my noticing
and out came someone who knew me better at 22 than I knew myself

I opened the confidante with whom I had been young — out came
a rugged photographer who listened and radiated a quiet kindness

I opened that kindness and attention and out came a supercharged
version of myself whose skin began to dance

I opened my skin to his and we became
a spray of sparks, starflash and second chances

Caridad Moro-Gronlier

neighborhood: Miami

nominated by (Mary Block)

In Defense of My Mother Who Never Bought Me a Barbie Dreamhouse

I was too young to understand
just how young my mother was
when she worked the nightshift
at TRW, building spacecrafts
with her hands, too young to know
how it felt to hand over the whole
of her check to my father
who gave her an allowance—
ten dollars after 40 hours,
ten dollars he'd drop into her palm
every pay day.

I understood Barbie called the shots.
That Dreamhouse was hers, Ken,
an accessory sans the authority
to tell her what to do.

I wrote thirty-one letters
to Santa that year,
but he wasn't in charge.

My father was.

I thought I stood a chance
because Mami loved Barbie's
mid-century mod A frame too,
how the chalet gleamed up at us
from the slick pages of the Sears catalog,

the wonder of real jalousie windows
and wall-to-wall carpets unfurled
on the kitchen table where she calculated
just how long she'd have
to lay that chalet away,
just how much she'd have to beg
to convince my father to pay.
I watched her turn the page,
no dogear to save her place.

I'd like to say I was happy
with the Barbie Dream Plane
she placed under the tree, but I blamed her.
It would take years to understand
she didn't want me to dream of staying put,
she wanted me to dream of flying away.

Originally published in *Limp Wrist*

Patio Pond Zoe Tribley

Mia Leonin

neighborhood: Miami

nominated by (Caridad Moro-Gronlier)

Creation Story

At age nineteen men translated my body for me:
You. Can't. Be. White. You

who got some extra lovin' on you. You,
ham hock booty.

On Troost Avenue, men rubbernecked and crashed,
a five-car pile up from looking at my ass.

And me – head down, eyes glued to cracked sidewalk
face hot with shame. And me –
wearing a red, A-line skirt that hit mid calf.

Years later, my husband explains, You can't cover that up.
A year after, a lover explains, Men know what's there,
even if they can't see it. That's their second sight, their sixth sense.

Southern folk translated my body for me.
Then Cubans did. *Criollita original!*
Negra vestido de blanco!
Gracias a la virgin por este culo.
From construction hangars, convertibles, and solares,
they hissed and whined and moaned.

I took a good, long look at my face:

my honey-splattered face, my cowrie-shell face, my calculus-meets-
physics face, my Neptune-trined-with-Saturn face, my split-second,
gut-instinct, don't-go-with-him face, my Venus-in-Cancer face, my

wanna-burn-every-war-monger-at-the-stake face, my wanna-nurse-every-baby-ever-racked-with-hunger face, my Yeah, I'm-buying-condoms. What-the-fuck-are-you-staring-at? face, my Uh huh, I-wanna-have-sex-and-I'm-not-interested-in-reproduction-so-dispense-with-the-dirty-looks-and-write-the-prescription face, my wanna-put-every-war-monger-on-trial face, my wanna-strip-down-naked-and-stand-in-front-of-a-military tank face, my ven-pa'ca-porque-te-quiero-comer face, my abandonment-issues-for-days face, my inner-child-before-it-was-a-pop-psychology-term face, my cowardly face, my fear-of-retribution face, my please-don't-take-this-little-piece-of-mountain-I've-managed-to-molehill-into-a- beautiful-windowsill-garden face, my I'm-through-with-molehilling face, my turns-out-I-am-the-mountain face.

I took a long, long look at my face
and I decided that it was good.

So I tossed that that mug, that kisser, that visage,
I tossed her to the horizon for safe keeping.

I fixed my gaze on her and I started walking.
This was the beginning of resting bitch face.

Originally published in *Grabbed: Poets and Writers on Sexual Assault, Empowerment, and Healing*

Jen Karetnick

neighborhood: Miami Shores

nominated by (Caridad Moro-Gronlier)

Insects

are extra food, we local women post every chance we get,
a shroud of swallows and thrushes around us as we jog
around the block at dusk. Sprays equal death. We would
make every tanager and grosbeak a gazpacho of flea and

mosquito if we could, force-feed them a ubiquitous
saveur of midges to go with beakfuls of extracted berries.
We judge, we jury those who hold biohazardous bottles over
grapefruit or key limes, we pluck the caterpillars from trees

too juvenile to meet the appetite of a hoard in order to recolonize
another inadequate backyard, though we know it can be difficult
to identify, exactly, what you're encouraged to cultivate when
you're both weight and gauge. Nurture the butterfly. Egg on

on a dragonfly, buoy up ladybugs. But plant-juicing thrips?
Jovial swarms of gnats? Quintuplicating ants? All sacrificial,
whiz-banging into flocks murmurating with such abrupt, judicious
turns you can't do anything but watch, struck by axial snacks

taken on the wing. The passerine head to points south, south
even of here where hundreds of thousands of Texans and New
Yorkers journeyed to find real estate with a water view during
quarantine. Life-size migration, a steady V, hardly as quaint

as dark-eyed juncos choosing our lawns for a meal of army worms
and wasps, a chorus of approval, and a doze. Snowbirds place
feeders on live oak limbs, surprised when colossal iguanas gulp
every goody and crawl Biscayne's bisque-like bay, when foxes

jump out from the undergrowth to eat the kibble left for the cat,
when even an acequia can hold an alligator. *Amazing*, they murmur,
then fertilize the yard and buy an extended warranty. We warn them:
We are bellyful, we are melody-ready, we are equipped for the haul.

Originally published in *The Dodge*

Catherine Esposito Prescott

neighborhood: Miami

nominated by (Jen Karetnick)

6 AM

Our electric car hums.
My boys drape their eyelids
over unfinished dreams.

The sun is a rumor. The sky blinks
with hunters, warriors, and every human's fate,
ancient mappings of this world,

which my boys would never accept
as truth unless it were proven in a TED Talk
or a self-appointed scholar's YouTube video.

My boys are a ram and a twin,
one thinks the other is his mate,
the other is stubborn and solitary.

I would tell them as much,
but they're not listening; their eyes
turn in and out of sleep.

As we approach the bus stop,
the car is stone-quiet. Before they walk
away, I want to say something

like carpe diem but wittier,
like This moment is all we have, but less alarmist,
like Be both the lion and the lamb.

I want to speak in metaphors

and aphorisms that will bloom in their minds
during third period, to singe them with grace.

This morning, I'm searching
for a phrase that's both spark and amulet,
but the silence between us

insists on staying empty
like a bowl of air carrying
the gentle charges of neutrons, electrons,

and protons, deeper quarks
and nucleons, the atomic and subatomic strata
pulsing inside layered atoms,

every energetic particle
moving in its own orbit,
maintaining an essential distance

from the others, so the entirety
doesn't collapse. These are distances
we have yet to measure--

the boys and I, and the world
outside, the invisible threads of all
I must leave unsaid.

From the book *Accidental Garden* (Gunpowder Press, February 2023), winner of the 2022 Barry Spacks Prize Originally published in *Nelle Journal* and reprinted in *Verse Daily*

Mary Block

neighborhood: Miami

nominated by (Rita Maria Martinez)

After Rebmann and the Safari Collection Brochure

Like a bird in a restaurant
I've been transformed
by the walls around me
into a filthy thing,
a hovering problem
who moves too fast
and doesn't know how to leave.

Like the 10-foot alligator caught
in a Clearwater kitchen,
hissing and thrashing around
in a puddle of red wine and glass,
I've been monstrously wrong.
My fury's gone viral.
My body's been made absurd
for its size and its suffering,
made available to subscribers.

Like the herd of giraffes
with their heads
through a hotel window
I want my beauty back.
I want to understand my rights
on either side of a given partition.
If a window implies permission,
turns me into a freaky background
for a stranger's vacation photos
I want to know.

Untitled by Iurii Laimin

Rita Maria Martinez

neighborhood: Miami

nominated by (Lenny DellaRocca)

I Write for Cyborgs and Shower Chair Users

I write to discover why my head thumps on the right,
not the left when weather plays Russian roulette.
I write to elude Lady Depression who pursues me
like a tenacious tabloid reporter, to transcend confines
of an aching vessel, to venerate this body despite its going
on strike over a week following the Covid vax, to honor ribs
that felt kicked in after, to praise caregivers like my spouse
whose steady hands unspooled a roll of camo-blue kinesio
tape over said ribs making me feel like an Olympic swimmer
in our blue sheets though I could barely roll over.
I humble myself before the majesty of adjustable beds,
revere my splendid Tempur-Pedic, its righteous remote
that gently raises and positions with a mere button push.
This is the closest I've come to living like the Jetsons.
I'm holding out for the George Jetson bathing experience:
almost sentient motion-detecting shower heads and jets
anticipating every need as I'm washed, rinsed, dried,
moisturized to perfection. For now I'm content
with the underappreciated shower chair, brush my teeth
while seated as my spouse lathers my back and hair.
I esteem the shower chair that welcomes and receives me
during post-migraine hangover when I'm unsteady.
I write to vent after watching The New Adventures of Old Christine
because Christine's ex-hubby and coworker mock her
asking if she's going to need a shower chair.
Why does society assume only the elderly use shower chairs?
I write to vanquish my timid younger self, obliterate

her fear of offending elders when mother advised silence,
to annihilate ableist statements disguised as advice.
I write for Paula Kamen's Tired Girls, exhausted women
inwardly rolling their eyes when asked if they've tried
yoga or acupuncture, for those with chronic daily headache
and migraine living in Florida where it's humid and hot
as fuck. For spoonie sisters fed some doozies:
You should mow the lawn. You like being sick.
Being tired is a state of mind. I write for those who use
MAOIs, CGRPs, NSAIDs. I pay tribute to legions
of responsible opioid users—chronic pain patients deemed
suspicious, often treated like drug-seeking addicts in ERs.
I write for the modified: cyborgs who loathe metal
detectors, borgs boasting internal or external hardware,
implanted with neurostimulators combating back pain,
incontinence, never-ending migraines.
I write because I'm a cyborg.

Originally published in a 2022 folio titled *A Forum on Disability and Poetics*—curated by
Christopher Salerno for *Tupelo Quarterly*

Rick Campbell

neighborhood: Alligator Point

nominated by (Lenny DellaRocca)

A Thousand Miles from Della Rose

When little I remember survives
this life will at last be mine.
As I stand in the valley, I know now
I'll have to tell you of our loss.
Your grandmother, the Rose of your name,
is gone. This valley that made me has gone
to another life. The dark cold mills, singing
of our lost gods and their slaughter block of dreams,
line the river like pallbearers. You'll think
I made too much of this, and I'll tell you all too often
of things you'll never see--forge, foundry,
furnace, the black smoke and slag.
Your land is loblolly and magnolia.
No coal barges crawl through your dreams.
We trade steel for flowers.
You are my new river.

Donald Morrill

neighborhood: Tampa

nominated by (Rick Campbell)

Blue Star Home

The blue star displayed in a house window means
knock on this door
if you're chased by a bully
or shadowed from school by a stranger in a car;
someone will answer,
will know what to do;
the world as you've felt it will remain so;
you're welcome,
don't forget.

But we do forget
even as we pound furiously for help,
or stroll past, imitating, on a plastic recorder,
a mourning dove.
Or living too deep in the back rooms,
out for the day,
we don't hear.
What was that?

When we answer
and discover that child in the frightened eyes
of a colleague, or our reflection,
we may bid it enter.
Before closing the door behind it, we peer out
for the threat,
for veracity (we've been tricked before,
we showing the star).
And there's our street. There's a maple leaf, fallen,
wide as a breastplate.

Originally published in *The Southern Review* and in Donald's book *At the Bottom of the Sky*

Brook J. Sadler

neighborhood: Tampa

---

nominated by (Donald Morrill)

White Horse Running Loose

I want to turn a white horse running loose on a highway overpass
in the south of France—
its white mane streaking against the blue sky
like a mythic messenger loosed from Olympus
and sent with the full intent of a rankled Zeus
or jealous Athena to speed the course of human events
toward conclusions we unwitting mortals would drive right by—

I want to turn a white horse running loose on a highway overpass
in the south of France—
its white gallop against the traffic
like a medieval ghost charging forth, its rider fallen,
emerging from the centuries as from battle,
clouds rising behind it like the smoke of a burned village,
bearing its noble purpose to fulfill some troubadour's forgotten promise—

I want to turn a white horse running loose on a highway overpass
in the south of France—
its dark nostrils like two coals,
legs and hooves like pistons, eyes glossy as volcanic glass,
muscled motion fluid as a wave's crest, curl, and final
unfurl, rolling toward shore, momentum that exhausts
and renews itself without pause—

I want to turn a white horse running loose on a highway overpass
in the south of France into a symbol in a poem,
but I cannot get a fix on it.
We were driving at 90 km/h, when it appeared above us,
a momentary flash, and it was gone.
A rift in the universe had opened and quickly sealed,
leaving only this recollection, wild, unbridled.

Boca by Renzo Del Castillo

Judy Ireland

neighborhood: West Palm Beach

nominated by (Lenny DellaRocca)

Eternal Graffiti

"Poetry is the eternal graffiti written on the heart of everyone."
—Lawrence Ferlinghetti

The heartless have dollar bills and cars with shiny rims
        mid-rib & to the left of center,
unlike lovers whose breastbones bristle with songs of songs,
        growing daily

five-o'clock poetry shadow. The lovers feel the spray-paint bursts
        like breezes,
rioting primary colors deepening as they dry into fattened words
        and gaudy flowers,

names of beloved cities, old schools, letters scrunched and styled,
        given highlights,
shadows, significance. The heartless fork over their inner trash bins,
        sorting

and grooming their useless crash of lung-squeezing junk,
        paying for stuff
no one wants. The lovers feel their inner bumper cars racing
        and the laughter --

their diaphragms riding waves of laughter. They memorized
        their poems before they
were born, and know them by heart.
        The heartless stay in their tiny rooms,

reading papers, watching their stocks balloon, no verse
        to hang a hat on, no song
to prop open a door, just a TV and a chair, a bowl
        on a side table with no fruit.

Elizabeth Jacobson

neighborhood: Lake Worth Beach

nominated by (Lenny DellaRocca)

Quantum Foam

The air is close by the sea and the glow from the pink moon
drapes low over a tamarind tree.

We hold hands, walk across a road rushing with traffic
to an abandoned building site on the bay, look out across the dark marina.

Sea cows sleep by the side of a splintered dock, a cluster of them
under the shallow water,

their wide backs covered in algae like mounds of bleached coral.

Every few minutes one floats up for air,
then drifts back down to the bottom,

without fully waking.
They will do this for hours, and for a while we try to match

our breath to theirs, and with each other's.

In the morning, sitting in the garden beneath thatch palms,
we drink black coffee from white ceramic cups.

Lizards killed by feral cats are scattered on the footpath.
I sweep them into a pile with the ones from the night before.

Waves of heat rise from the asphalt,
and we sense a transparent gray fuzz lightly covering everything

as if there were no such thing as empty space,
that even a jar void of substance holds emptiness as if it were full.

Originally published by the Academy of American Poets *Poem-a-Day*

Gulf by Gina Moriarty

Yael Valencia Aldana

neighborhood: Pompano Beach

---

nominated by (Lenny DellaRocca)

To Watch Her Face Fall

I.

I am wounded
my washi thin skin darkens with blood
frayed open flesh ragged
at the edges. I don't want
to tell her, to show her—
but she will ask.

I can bear it alone, the weight of this upset, knit
the lesion back before I see her,
continue the interlacing of fascia after
I see her, conceal the bruise
the sliced skin—
but she will ask.

I harrow then sear watching her face crest and fall
watching her shining shadow. If only for a few
minutes till her face brightens,
till her mouth dances to distract
from my harm.

Our love is this silent chaffing.

II.

Bodily harm becomes invisible shadowing
barely darkened imperfections, a closing
over that will smooth—

return to unblemished perfection
to all eyes but ours, only us aware
of the slight scar lightly covered in hair.
Smoothing over her face that fell.

She cannot forgive because it was me
I cannot forgive because it was her—
her face that fell.

She wants to go back. Soothe
with words as slim as apple chips.
Soothe with her rhythmic voice
that rises and falls in waves.

Our faces slick over, leaving only slight
sharpening in the corners of the shields
in our eyes squinting, glinting
black metal.

She will say it's alright and not mean it
I will agree and not mean it.

We will put our glossy heads together,
draft new plans for unnamed streets.

She will hold my hand tighter
which is the only good bit. Until I am ready
to leave the hearth of her protection
sheathed in armor we will temper
anew.

Originally published in *Superstition Review*

Woman with Lemon by Oladimeji Odunsi

Clayre Benzadón

neighborhood: Coconut Grove

nominated by (Yael Valencia Aldana)

Moon as Salted Lemon

tonight I wedge
the moon
into bottom
of glass

con cada luna llena

watch it erupt
leak teal
cuando llega
el atardecer

I can't squeeze
Julieta Venegas'
"Limon Y Sal" out

of my head
only Clase Azul
finger-
tip swirling
salt around
the rim

of a shotglass

Evening brings out
the bluest part

almost half
of this lemonmilk

body is salted
by silicon
dioxide glass
created by meteoroids
hitting it

Originally published in *SWWIM Every Day*

Susan L. Leary

neighborhood: Coral Gables

nominated by (Clayre Benzadón)

Dressing the Bear

for Brittany

This time, we give the body shoes. The body of a bear
my brother is building at a factory in the mall to give
to the girl he's loved since the sixth grade. I'm there to pay
for the bear & to speak of none of it, which is fine
because I'm good at hiding the ways my brother has wanted.
This time is different. At each station, my brother stuffs
only the good parts of himself inside the slack fur.
He gives the bear perfumed bones & shiny gold laces
& breathes so as not to snap them. He considers what the girl
wants & I consider his face as he forgets he has one,
as if in loving the girl & loving her limb by clothed limb,
for once, my brother can love himself. Probably,
that bear is in a Florida landfill, barefoot & decapitated,
its floral button-down shirt torn & full of crawfish stains.
But the girl arrives at my brother's service in a blue & pink
striped dress, a burst skeleton of human sky—& I remember
the air as we exited the mall that day, the reddest bomb
of a fist before us. Then my brother, with insight delicate
enough not to wreck the evening: It's harder to catch
the sunrise, he says. You have to really want it.

Originally published in *Up the Staircase Quarterly* and in Susan's book, *Dressing the Bear* (Trio House Press)

Daily Bread by Andrew Rader Hanson

Andrew Rader Hanson

neighborhood: Delray Beach

nominated by (Alexa Doran)

Twentynine-Palms

December rasp, dust in stream,
lust of color illumined. The dealer
smears the stars & splits
a stone decked & assembled
by yesterday's air. Tumbleweeds
gambol sunward, & in the dusk,
by their shadows, weave the sky
into the sand--

Alexa Doran

neighborhood: Tallahassee

nominated by (Susan L. Leary)

At the Roller Rink, You Remind Me of Your Mother

how certain she is I'm an owl, the most haunted of the birds; warned
you: wide berth - but you're so sure you've never seen me fly, no beak
prey-deep, no talon-pale leaves, no wonder to write against the sky, that you
assure me she's blind. I wonder if this is how Snow White felt, forced to fuck
her life away in a cabin, to make song of ash in the ass of some mountain,
all because another woman couldn't find a way to future her own fountain.
Neon lights rhythm the rink and I watch you watch my son Grestky my
ankles as we spin. Is this in your mother's vision? My son's weight balanced
between us, his hand learning to trust through the rough of your touch. Oh,
to be a plum ice bidden from the box, enormous with glisten and bloated
by snowdrop, ready for the thistle of jaw – instead of here, tossed like
marshmallow on the bonfire of your fears, my melt the only thaw. Does she
weep knowing we fall asleep, my fingers spelling battles into the fault line of
your teeth, my thighs dragging your mouth like a saw?

William May

neighborhood: Boca Raton

nominated by (Lenny DellaRocca)

Our Plan Did Not Go Well

and the things we did instead
were nothing I wanted,
did not satisfy any of those desires.
I am still trapped with them,
and they will not relent,
will continue to demand
what was anticipated,
what has been denied.
I know, it is impossible
to change this, to have it.
The chance was missed
and it is gone, will not return.
It is the way of things,
but I am still waiting.
I do not know
how to let go of it.
I want to make it better
and not have it be one more thing
that has gone all wrong
and cannot be corrected.

Gregory Byrd

nominated by (Lenny DellaRocca)

Theory of Gravity

Imagine you wake at five thirty to a DJ's careful voice.
You turn on a bedside lamp and on the wall, a damselfly
as if in space, weightless.
Perhaps it came in with the cats,
perhaps when you did, maybe through some small entrance
in your falsely tight house.
You know you should trap it in a whiskey glass--
in a little dome of pure alcoholic air--
slide a postcard from Paraguay beneath its weightless feet
and carry it to the back door where it could rise
into the dawning sky.
You have faith in your own gentleness,
reach for the little folded wings,
use them as a simple handle.
But as if to confirm that even your most benign motions
are murderous without compassion,
your fingers clutch the thread-thin body as well,
crush it in your most gracing grip.
Even in your cupped hands
it tears against your calluses.
When you reach the back porch and the starred morning sky
and let the thing loose, it only struggles into the air,
pitching and dipping--no longer a predator
but a perfect opportunity for a quick bird
to take it further into the sky.
And imagine then that you fly to your brother's bedside,
listen to his wife talk about morphine drips and radiation,
that you tell her to go home and sleep.

You see his closed eyes move
as if they were something trying to escape.
You hold his thin hand
as if your breath could break it,
as if you were the one who could let him out.

Originally published by *Tampa Review* and in Gregory's book, *Salt and Iron*, (Snake Nation Press, 2014)

Meryl Stratford

neighborhood: Hallandale Beach

nominated by (Lenny DellaRocca)

Her Education

Into the quiet classroom
of the mind comes flying
the furious teacher with a lesson
of fear. This bullet
is not a bullet, it's merely
a word, something the mouth
makes for the delicate ear,
something the breath sends
that troubles the air, a ballet
of sound moving through silence
that explodes in an image as sudden
as death. Where is the wound?
It bleeds in the minds of a million
grief-stricken girls. They will be
pilots, doctors, warriors,
poets. They will sit on the ground
in the dust, just to learn.

Originally published in the anthology *Malala: Poems for Malala Yousafzai* (FutureCycle Press, 2013)

P. Scott Cunningham

neighborhood: Miami

nominated by (Anjanette Delgado)

Qasida of the Pinecone
after Lorca

The pinecone
wasn't asking for the dawn:
almost undead on its limb,
it asked to be alone.

The pinecone
wasn't asking for science or shadow:
the mind's and body's limits,
it asked to be alone.

The pinecone
wasn't asking for the pinecone:
the stillness of the sky was in it;
it asked to be alone.

Originally published in *Ya Te Veo* (University of Arkansas, 2018)

Untitled by Sean E. Sexton

Campbell McGrath

neighborhood: Miami

nominated by (P. Scott Cunningham)

Sebastian

Central Florida,
cows and orange trees and grass—
not much to look at.

Healing—the way cracks
in certain country roads are
sutured with asphalt.

Indian River—
white egret stalking the reeds,
solitude!—and joy!

Mosquitoes? No sir,
not here, you must be thinking
of Alabama.

Flowers, no flowers,
I've forgotten everything
but the ebb and flow.

Exist like a snail,
just *be*—one small galaxy
of human purpose.

Untitled by Marquise Kamanke

Gabrielle Aboki

neighborhood: Tallahassee

nominated by (Zuleyha Ozturk Lasky)

Mario's Last Dance

The doors of the church swung open,
and sunlight kissed our skin, welcomed us
to the realities of the new world
no more smile in my uncle's eyes.

That unholy morning, my aunt called
to tell my grandmother she had lost
her son on her birthday, Bible slipped
from her fingers as she cursed into the open air.

My uncle, who surprised me with bright
pink rolls of Bubble Tape gum and UNO,
who was the first to jump on the dance floor
at a wedding reception, a crowd always watching,

not unlike that night outside of The Gambler.
The gunshots pierced the air, shattering
through bone, his skull—a wine glass
falling from careless hands.

How cold his body must have felt
when the crowd scattered and left him
alone on the 3 a.m. concrete to die
in darkness, barely making it to Sunday.

Zuleyha Ozturk Lasky

neighborhood: Tallahassee

nominated by (Max Lasky)

We Fuel Us Clairvoyant

We take off our headscarves. We shut blinds. We take wing
    after wing and boil us. We burn paper as fuel for the samovar.
    We no longer pray in mosques, we no longer sin, instead we king

our sky as clairvoyant. Break our bones like reeds to sing
    until we return to Medusa's mausoleum. Our hands appear
    to take off our headscarves. We shut blinds. We take wing

after wing: burn over sky, we snow us in—a mother sting
    in our womb. We bury Istanbul. We forget our wooden hair.
    No longer we pray. No longer we sin in mosques. Instead, we king

our grandmother gutting peppers. We pocketknife. We shrink
    our sky as clairvoyant. We pluck our lives. We chore. We tear.
    We take off the blinds and shut our heads. Scarfed, we break wing

after chicken wing cooked beside stuffed peppers we bring
    us to clairvoyance. We burn joyous. We wear tight the fear
    of mosques. Prayers tell us to no longer sin. Instead, we king

ourselves. We exist in every story censored, every surgical string
    to enclose us. We milk us sour and burn us as fuel for the samovar.
    We take off our headscarves. We shut their blinds. Take our wings
off no mosque prayers. We sin longer! No longer do we king.

originally published in *Small Orange*

Max Lasky

neighborhood: Tallahassee

nominated by (Colin Callahan)

A Ghost's Proposal in a Court

You handed her a ring while the rain slanted
then turned aside. She vetted the thing
like a veteran jeweler, eyes dialed in
under the streetlight's hum as you stood
against her car in a cul de sac. Who drove
a nail into your palm? Holding the stone
upturned in one hand, she appraised the world:
the band was stained, ring head cut of amethyst,
and the rain fell constant, cold like a chorus
to some lame pop song she always sung
now stuck in your head. She thought then
you couldn't trust, even if you sometimes did
momentarily, sporadically—it was a problem.
When you caught scent of seasalt, fishbait,
you recalled all those summers never coming
back again, standing near the Broadway Basin—
the same fishing charters, docked in predawn,
pass through the Manasquan Inlet by daybreak,
the inlet connecting the river to the ocean,
the rough Atlantic. Before she could respond
first light broke low, some gulls flew overhead.
She wishes you were sober, she said, cleaner
than sand in glass, warm as the warmest sunrays
straying in through windshield, across the wheel,
and you agreed. Twirling the ring in your hand,
you were half happy she declined and didn't say
how you read into signs that don't exist, at least
to no one except you—the gull swooping low

from a street pole means more than its cries,
that she's close, for instance, to being hopeless,
or that you have a chance if you start charting
the right path. And later, wordless on a bench,
you watched a row of people along the seawall,
some casting their lines out, others reeling in,
and one untangling his from a stranger's.
You considered throwing the ring into the water,
you thought of handing it off to someone random,
of hocking it at the nearest pawn shop just if
the profit was worth it. She'll either miss you
or she won't. And though the view of the ocean
was wider than the quiet court she grew up on,
more expansive with the clouds plowing over
the horizon, the cut up surface glinting
shards of diamond, nothing inside your chest
swelled or opened, nothing broke like a wave
or ebbed, your desire heading in two directions
like the ships through the inlet, some to harbor,
others seaward, and you, steady in the middle.

Collin Callahan

neighborhood: Tallahassee

nominated by (Kate Sweeney)

Dear Corporation

Richard and I knife the moonrocks
into separate piles
on a mattress hidden in the skimp forest outline
of an industrial park.
They crackle like rat skulls
in the blades of a lawnmower.
Richard squiggles warmblood
horses on a napkin
as I rock back and forth like a machine
full of wet clothes.
Moths powder the handrails of gaunt stairwells.
This light has the quality
of a midwestern hospital.
Nitrous canisters lie about.
I think about submarine warfare
and those balloons in the dead girl's backyard.
The electrical plant is pink thunder.
I tuck the aluminum foil into my breast pocket
like a beautiful child.

Originally published in *Bat City Review* where it was featured as the winner of the
2021 Bat City Review Editor's Prize in Poetry.

Burrowing Owl by Cleiton Silva

Sidney Wade

neighborhood: Gainesville

nominated by (Sarah Carey)

Burrowing Owl

Very odd,
this little cloud

in trousers
in the sandy

fortress
favored by

prairie dog
and gopher

tortoise.
On the mound

at the mouth-hole,
he scouts around

with sybilline
yellow eyes

and then, owl-
wise, decides

to clean house.
He dives down

and soon
great clouds

of smudge come
flying out,

his home now
clean as a bone.

A diurnal owl,
he's upside-down

and inside-out,
at ease

not in trees,
but underground,

where his mate
broods

on her eight
fragile moons

in an immaculate
burrow whose

contours are lined
with cow manure.

Sarah Carey

neighborhood: Gainesville

nominated by (Jen Karetnick)

A Pileated Woodpecker Shares Where to Find God

I live for what the dead give.

Hidden by leaf screens and branches,
I pillage rotting wood. My tribe fought
long for salvation, after the forests' razing,

dug into ragged stumps, felled trunks--
a miracle of wholeness from fragments,
a feast of insects who thrive on decay.

What's left when I leave is for others to say.

Should you see my black wings
and red head knocking wood for nourishment,
you might ask if I believe God is dead,

as Altizer said, that God lived and died
in Christ, that the church lied
about becoming the body—but what Altizer said

was not what most thought he meant,
he really meant in death, life—a spirit
indwelling to drill the dying down,
incarnate carnage, God's passion.

If you ask me, I'm proof he was right.

If you listen to my rat-a-tat melody

echoing my drumming beak, you may hear
an answered prayer of oneness in desire's

shrill tattoo, and the thrumming
of your own wild heart.

Originally published in *SWWIM Everyday*

David Axelrod

neighborhood: Vero Beach

nominated by (Lenny DellaRocca)

A Great Spirit
(Winnipesaukee translates to "smile of the great spirit.")

The chill of September
lake water challenges me.
It always takes extra will
power to set my feet down
blindly feeling soft mud
squeeze between my toes,
lowering myself as cold
water reaches my bathing
suit. The diving raft, twenty
yards out, was a long swim
for me at ten. Even now,
accustomed to ocean's
buoyancy, I sink quickly,
but without the little kid's
moment of urgency wishing
for an adult hand to pull
me up. As a little kid, I'd
make a silly self-dare that I
could make the swim unaided
and not be some sickly kid.
From what I learned from
asthma, struggling for air
wasn't a heroic thing. Granted,
my mother used to tell me
"Someday, you will be better."
Of course, she meant medically
weller, but the opposite of
"better" meant I must be bad.

Here I was, returning at
middle age and I still heard
echoes taunting me that
it would serve me right
if I drowned. How long
before I'd be found in the
dark water? I heard a fellow
had filled his pockets with rocks
and when they finally found
him, fished him out, he was
blue and bloated. Maybe it was
all the dark water he swallowed.
I was the kind of kid who worried
about what was in the lake water.
We joked, "Fish piss in it." Now,
I know diatoms, not pollution, tint
the water dark. But the thought
of a vastly-deep spot still conjures
wisps of my disappearing.

Kids know the boogeyman is
real. He's the real reason
people vanish. To be daredevils,
adults learn to take risks,
but most kids take unknowing
chances. Panicked by a need
to live, as a kid I couldn't,
as I do now, breaststroke
upward, roll on my back
for a deep breath, stretch out
and stroke toward the weathered
raft lightly rocking as I stroke
toward it to climb the wood
ladder. Bright sun bakes
the initial chill away.

I savor a few minutes
lying back, eyes closed. I stand
to dive in again, checking
to be sure it's deep enough to
leap headfirst without fear
of a broken neck. Poor Billy
in my grade school who was
paralyzed for not checking.
Even then I thought, "Who
could live like that? Nothing
you could do? I would rather
die." And he did die a dozen
years later, never again
shouting, as we kids did,
"Mommy, watch me."

My mother would tell me
that when I reported whatever
prejudice or cruelty,
"There's nothing we
can do." Once, when
a neighbor kid split my
scalp open with a rock,
my parents couldn't even
get his parents to pay for
stitches. Early on, I knew
things could be worse than
death. If death took you,
maybe it ended your pain.

Swimming off the raft,
no one is close enough
to save me or even notice
if I let myself go under

to drown. I've checked in
to the cabin alone, said nothing
to a soul except the cabin's owner
whom I see is way down shore
tending to business.

My parents would bring me
here for a week-long vacation
in the foothills of the White
Mountains. By late summer,
evenings were already putting
a chill into the lake. They would
rent a musty cabin, maybe
from this same fellow's dad.
We'd have a sitting room
with a kitchen counter,
two bedrooms with army
blankets over stiff sheets
on hard mattresses
suspended on mesh chains.

Not even enough sand along
the steep lake shore for a kid
to fill a pail, scraping with
a blue plastic shovel.
Back home, we lived by
the ocean where there was
plenty of sand. Why come
here except my folks would
say, "Let's get away." We'd
pack the Oldsmobile for a long
ride, with me asking, "Are we
there yet?" culminating with
sandwiches for supper, early

bedtime. For me, nothing to do
for those vacation days was
still better than starting school.
Ma could ignore cooking
except to slap together
peanut butter and jelly,
or boil hotdogs. My Dad
could take a break from
wrecker calls and engine
breakdowns, his skills
focused on a one-lung
Evinrude for fishing in
the center of the lake where
we caught an occasional
pickerel. Never anything
as grand as a bass. A family
vacation—better than kids
I pitied whose parents
sent them off to sleep-over
camp. At the lake, I'd wheeze
from ragweed, but I could
venture out alone, wade
through primrose though I
did need to be cautious not
to let it catch my ankles.
Avoid the bulrush, snap off
a cattail that could mimic a whip
or serve as my mock cigar as
I wondered why life was hard.
Seventy years later, I'm still
trying to solve what some
joke is "the mystery of life."

Maybe it was actually
hiding all this time with

the great spirit deep in
the dark waters. I decide
to dive and touch the bottom.
I twist upward, break the surface,
scissor kick. Far less gasping
and drama than when I was barely
able to make it on my own.
Again, I climb up, tuck my toes
over the edge, do an acceptable
arc into cold water. I frog
kick back to the ladder
to climb up again, letting
eddies run down my sides,
trickle on my inner thighs
like a kid who has peed his
bathing suit. "A fish will
bite you there," we'd laugh
skinny dipping in a secluded
spot near my home. And now,
just me nearly eighty in an old
bathing suit. But why wear
anything at all? Okay, the law,
or mischievous fish who'd
yank at me. Better wear this
suit to cover what parts are
left of me though I'm equally
used up, blanched by too many
immersions. Still, I'm able to
cinch myself up on an exquisite
day. I remember when a friend
and I, building our own scrap-
wood raft, were nailing boards.
I hit my finger and the pain
was exquisite. I'd heard that
term "exquisite," for first
time at a matinee. A cowboy

said it. "Are you okay?" my
friend asked over my hollering
after I hit my finger. And I
had to say it, though he had
no idea what I meant: "The pain
is exquisite," but it sure took
a long time before the aching
stopped. Later, a big, blood
blister. But the nail grew back.

I've come back to Winnipesaukee
looking for signs the way
fortune tellers in ancient times
read augurs. An eagle rises from
pitch pines, slowly circles
the shore eying a rabbit. It's
not a water fowl, doesn't dive
or alight on water. I'm neither
osprey nor eagle—more likely
to duck than attack. I'm losing
height and weight, figuring
when and where to alight.
Hundreds of years of people
have swum here. How many
drownings, miscalculations,
"I can swim from here to there."
Or sudden seizures, lost
below the surface. There were,
certainly, people who stroked
far enough out to assure
their own death. Then,
there were also the winter
cracks on thin ice with
too-late hands pulling up
hypothermic, blue faces.

An afternoon-soft breeze has
quickened to an imminent
thunderstorm. I've known
those so true to their faith
or so heavily armed by habits
that they don't heed danger,
or simply can't shift plans
or change direction. I dive
toward the shore where I drape
a rough towel over my shoulders--
same as the cabins always had
only it covered more of me
when I was ten. I make it
inside the cabin just as large
drops let loose with a lightning
flash. I count—one thousand
one, one thousand two, one
thousand three. A boom.
I calculate the lightning
is a half mile away.
This old cabin, with its wide
boards nailed to true timber—
full 2 x 4s—will protect me
though it's uninsulated.
I've rented it for one night.
Time enough if I swim out
and simply sink. Instead,
I pull off my bathing suit,
rinse off in lukewarm water.
I treat myself to a second,
clean towel, pull up my
worn chinos.

Once, I was a sickly kid who
actually made it all the way
out alone, but hoping someone
would notice me. If my Ma
were there as I perched to dive,
I'd be crying, "Watch me."
Now, I see the brown water
thrashing the shore. Whitecaps
rise as the louder, more-rapid
thunder approaches. I could
rush out heedless, sink
or swim. I sit by a partly-
opened window to let
a wet wind blow in.
The fierceness of the storm
passes me by. I'm okay--
for a fact, I'm serviceable,
and still very much alive.

Heron by Airam Dato-on

Outback by Sean E. Sexton

Chris Bodor

neighborhood: St. Augustine

nominated by (Rita Maria Martinez)

Fierce, a Poem for My Future Granddaughter

Your mother made me a father
during a time when I was full of youth
during a time when I knew nothing
about marriage,
about making money,
about happiness.

You will make me a grandfather
and I will make mistakes
as a grandfather,
as I have as a father
as I have as a husband,
a brother, and a son.

The only gift I have to give you
for Christmas,
for the new year,
for your birthday,
is my love
and a Winston Churchill quote,
discovered on my writing desk,
in a 2023 monthly planner:

"You will make all kinds of mistakes,
but as long as you are generous and true,
and fierce, you cannot hurt the world
or even seriously distress her."

When you are born, future granddaughter,
I hope that you will take my hand,
and lead me through your world,
and teach me how to be fierce

Untitled by Sean E. Sexton

Steven Bradbury

neighborhood: Melrose

nominated by (Danny Lawless)

On the Eros of Their Conversation

If this is where we make our bed, he mused,
apropos of nothing they had said
but in answer to the latent question
around which they had played for hours like children
let from school, as they reveled in their near-
animal pleasure in the rough and tumble
of each other's conversation, so be it,
for is this not love's sweetest part? The gentle
art of letting your hair down over a verbal
pratfall, of falling into the arms of a ribald pun,
of peeling the layers off a juicy allusion that leaves
you lying in such a state of linguistic undress
that you begin to wonder where this talk will
take you, when all the words are finally gone.

Danny Lawless

neighborhood: Lake Worth

---

nominated by (Steve Kronen)

Freudenschreck

Freudenschreck, or "intense pleasure-fright"—leave it to the Germans
To coin a word for the fleeting sense of being seized
By such an inexplicable joy it verges on terror.
Or maybe it's inexplicable terror pretending to be joy.
Also, a physical phenomenon: neurologists say the amygdala
Glows red as a jack ball whether subjects gaze at images of planetesimals or
       gallows.
Picture a joyride, the Appalachian pin-brides of Eugene Meatyard.
Put yourself in the shoes Of Aiyana Clemmons, 44,
Of Peru, Indiana, a long-time congregant of the End Days
Christian Church according to the *Gazette*, *who* may have had a seizure
That caused her to "shiver all over" although another passerby reported
Hearing her shout "Praise Him!" or "Praise God!" before "she sort of
       rocked him"
Before casting that beautiful child into that cold river.

Untitled by Maria Lysenko

Geoffrey Philp

neighborhood: Miami

nominated by (Holly Iglesias)

A Daughter of Oshún
(after Kwame Dawes)

I am a daughter of Oshún.
I can coax green from dead wood,
a fury of stalks from a single seed
that brings a farmer to his knees,
chanting orikis in praise of my breasts.
And when I've finished my work for the day,
I come alive when the bangarang begins.
On the dance floor, old men drop
their walking sticks to skank to my beat,
rise from wheelchairs for a dutty wine.
For when I rub, when I dub,
when this sweetness, like juice
from a ripe naseberry covers my skin
and my thighs tremble, rum heads
leave their spirits and become
preachers of my word.

I am a daughter of Oshún.
The ample sway of my hips, this strut
that takes prisoners and releases them
(if they are lucky by the next morning)
has stopped husbands' hands in mid-air
as they were about to slap dominoes
on the table, scattering tiles into their partner's
laps, but out of respect for the delicacy
of my ears, they slide back into their chairs
and beg forgiveness. But I ignore their pleas,
fearing that I'll find them in my driveway,

waiting like stray cats under the papaya.

I am a daughter of Oshún.
Sister to the John Crow, eater of the dead
buried under cement and zinc in the streets
of Port-au-Prince, whose scent followed
me into the holy presence of my father
where I pleaded for mercy on my fellow travelers
on these roads where Oyá could not venture.
I dared to live despite the bitterness under my tongue.

Barbra Nightingale

neighborhood: Hollywood

nominated by (Geoffrey Philp)

The 18th Chili Dog
after Ashbery

It was summer
　or the end of summer
Indian Summer has gone out of fashion.
　Cancel culture and all that.

The skies at night are red and white streaked
　with blue, or checkerboard
like those papers in the basket
　at Boardwalk eateries.

There was a can waiting to be filled,
　a blank page waiting to be inked.
It all happens so suddenly
　it's hard to take it all in.

That's when the bell rings
　ending it all.
Or is it just the beginning?
　Look to the east.

Howard Richard Debs
neighborhood: Palm Beach Gardens

nominated by (Geoffrey Philp)

Dorian Before, During, After
"They worry about the silliest things, a little bit of wind"
— patron exiting the Brooklyn Bagel eatery, pre-storm, Palm Beach
Gardens, Florida

Her name is Lauren. She played her part.
More about that later. Humans give everything
names. *Wednesday August 28*: I'm putting up
the metal garage door center brace—a gaping chasm
if breached therefore it's fortified like a medieval castle
entry with its massive wooden gates fronted by its portcullis
(a vast iron grille to thwart storming by battering rams)
I'm not yet thinking I might die. I'm thinking of Dorian
columns (bearing the most weight ancient builders
used them at the base of buildings). I'm thinking
that Dorian will be ripped apart by the mountainous
terrain of Hispaniola. *Thursday August 29*: I'm putting up
the heavy galvanized steel shutters I invested in long ago
to cover all the windows and sliding glass doors. *Friday August 30*:
I'm bringing in all the furniture from the patio; anything
can be a missile even the small stone birdbath marking the
spot where we buried the container of our cat's remains when she died
of natural causes many years ago. I'm thinking it's coming our way.
Saturday August 31: I'm helping put up shutters at
my younger daughter's place; a first responder with Palm
Beach County Fire Rescue, she's activated at Emergency
Headquarters as of 7 a.m. the next day. The plan is we'll head
to her house, it's newer construction, post-Andrew, up-to-code.
One of her twins, eleven years old, complains it's dark inside
with all the windows covered. I'm thinking this will be the worst storm to hit our
area in 45 years since we moved to Florida for the
sea and sun of it. I later find out about the Labor Day hurricane
of 1935 and its 185 mile-an-hour winds. *Sunday September 1*:

I'm clinging to our only hope, waiting for *The Turn*.
(The Bermuda High came and retreated, leaving a smidgen
of room for the hurricane to skirt the coast, a low-pressure
trough coming down from the Midwest coaxing it along
if it reached us in time). *Monday September 2*: I'm packing
to leave my home. I'm thinking living generates lots of stuff,
as George Carlin used to joke ("If you didn't have so much stuff,
you wouldn't need a house, you could just walk around all the time.")—
I'm thinking I could lose it all, my stuff. The Hebrew *Daily Prayers* with
English translations passed down through generations take it or leave it?
The old black and white photo of Grandpa Eddie in front of his
haberdashery on Broadway in Chicago take it or leave it?
The leather-bound *Essays and Treatises on Several Subjects* by Hume,
1769 edition take it or leave it? *Tuesday September 3*: I'm reading
the latest Facebook post from my son-in-law, a local high school
history teacher with a passion for storm prediction. He previously
posted about his former student Lauren, now a meteorologist flying
on a hurricane hunter plane to gather data. Dorian is stalled.
We're all still waiting for *The Turn*. The delay is maddening with
possible devastating result (meme being circulated online: Dorian
is just like a Florida snowbird. It moves 1 mile an hour, can't pick a lane
and has no idea when to turn). Finally the 6z models, known as spaghetti
plots show movement to the northwest. Confidence is high that we will see
minimal effects. I call around, the big chain restaurants are closed but
a local diner opened and so instead of eating Sterno-heated instant oatmeal
we went out on the town. The place was packed with weary folks abuzz
about our salvation and the tragedy in the Bahamas 90 miles away. A fellow
at the next table was insisting we send all donations only to Christian-based
charities. I resisted a demurral. *Wednesday September 4*: I'm thinking I'm over
the mileage for an oil change on the new car; an email arrives from the
dealer reading "With Dorian behind us we're here for all your automotive
needs." I'm thinking of *Dorian Gray*, the novel.

Originally published in *Brown Bag*, Issue 1

Afterword--
Three things: 1). A number of years ago, in the *Michigan Quarterly Review* a group of
literary luminaries joined the fray in a series of seven articles about writing Holocaust
poetry. Alicia Ostriker had this to say, "Writing is what poets do about trauma. We
try to come to grips with what threatens to make us crazy, by surrounding it with

language." 2). When my older daughter, now a public school special education resource specialist started her undergraduate career at Florida State in Tallahassee, the parents were treated to a lecture to show the kind of thing the students would be experiencing. The history professor involved propounded a theory which is both profound and difficult involving a meta-analysis approach asserting that all events, devastating hurricanes included, have positive outcomes if viewed in a larger context. The point of view is hard to reconcile. 3). Climate change is an existential threat, yet, as with Dorian Gray, collectively we have given away our future in exchange for the enjoyments of the moment.

Formation by Sean E. Sexton

Michael Hettich

nominated by (Barbra Nightingale)

The Problem of Analysis

This city is so large, no one could possibly
walk every street in one lifetime, even
walking every day. In fact, this city
has grown so massive it might not even be
a city, properly speaking, but more like
the nerves and atoms in an ordinary brain
of someone who happens to be sleeping, let's say--

and if we could sneak inside her as she dreams,
stilling our breath not to wake her, we might
look more closely up and down the meandering
alleys, peer along the hallways and alcoves
of the buildings inside her, of the lives there—as now,
through a half-opened window on the second floor
a young man sits reading. When his phone rings,
he answers, distracted, looking down
at the street, where a beautiful woman is walking
a dachshund who poops in the middle of the sidewalk
while she pretends to examine her manicure,

which infuriates the young man, who tosses his phone
and leaps through the door to the street, to give her
a piece of his mind—which makes this a good time
to move in deeper, into another neighborhood,
where an old man who looks like a dog in a bathrobe
is pouring milk into a fish tank
crowded with pollywogs, or to a public swimming pool
where children are engaged in a race to see
how fast they can drink all its water. At the bottom

something is moving. And one boy, a show off,
keeps jumping from the diving board, trying to swim
to the bottom and touch that shape—whatever
it is—before it lies still. On another street,
trains full of feathers fly past waiting rooms;
someone gathers spider webs to make a violin
while caves are being dug in the ground behind the bleachers
by girls who were cheerleaders before they grew moss;

and still we move deeper, stealthily, growing
harder to see as it grows harder
to see ourselves anywhere, until we can't help
becoming more like the trees and birds
that sang here a thousand years ago than we are
like ourselves, dear city of the inner life,
until we are less than a smidgen of sap
that might once have quickened a now- extinct species
of flower that smelled like the sky, deep
in the layers and folds of our memories, where

we're nothing like ourselves, where bees still gather
pollen with a buzzing that fills the afternoon
wherever that afternoon is, and pollinate
other long-extinct flowers to make
honey as sweet as this brief time we've been given

to breathe.

Untitled by Austin Ellis

Sarah Carleton

neighborhood: Tampa

nominated by (Pamela Epps)

Flood Zone

Back porch, black sky, bugs as big as tadpoles fly
close to one light bulb, flick and bap
to the pulse of pond frogs.

We lounge one step from underwater in this sub-sand
altitude where alligators stumble drunk
into backyards

led by primordial memories of submerged land
and baffled to be breathing pure
sodden oxygen

so let's acclimate ourselves to this place from the inside
out, get soused on margaritas and tea
till our heads swim--

let's drink and dream until the walls bend, until catfish
weave through louver windows
until we grow gills.

First published in *Valparaiso Poetry Review* (Spring/Summer 2021, Vol. XXII, No. 2)

C.M. Clark

neighborhood: Sebastian

nominated by (Sean Sexton)

Next to Last Chance Saloon

Halfway between cow and cormorant
Lake Wales appears. Your perfect excuse
to quit driving. To quit
the keener purpose of driving
between what is boundless and the finite. Always
the ground between.
An off-road shoulder like some old woman's bed
growing colder with years and indifferent. Can you imagine
the sheer acreage of exfoliating skin?

The body scent that fades
with each day's exhalation? Or are you called instead
inside a virtual elsewhere, the echoed jackhammer of feet
up
dizzying hexagons of tiled stairways?
Migraine-blind you rise
six flights. But the back bedroom stays hidden--
just waiting behind dry cleaning and winter coats
cocooned and swaddled in plastic. These

are the places that joust, that beckon
east to west, taking refuge and a lunch
where avoidance is most likely preferred
offering either
chicken fried steak or breakfast all day. Or
just the jazz
of numbing hours
and miles, just
for the lust of soft Gulf water.

There is a dead spot I like
between points on the map.
Still too close to the town receding
as only a vague blur of slow traffic
and low buildings fixed

in the rearview mirror. Yet
not yet near enough the next county line --
not yet my destination -- yet a welcome
relief from the monotony
of brush and flat field.

In this dead spot I spin the dial.
Still a younger sister to radio days, knowing
the place by the cellphone towers.
Better than the billboards,
the come-to-Jesus vowels crooning

the oldies, the country quick nod
to God and Sunday.
But here
in the dead
spot

I snag only fragments of a place
already distant, and even fewer
half sentences anticipating
the next exit
still out beyond my windshield.

Straining to hear the transmissions
of forgettable voices straining
to assemble some meaningful
message, although every third word is swallowed
within the blur of road noise and wind shear.

From here to your front door due west
pavement plumbs the numbing miles.
The succinct limits of my very human vision –
my old tired eyes – the tired blue – succumbing
to cataract fog and still
straining west, the still unseen outpost
on your coast beyond my best attempt
to conjure you in your kitchen, closing
lower cupboards, with a brisk hip move.

The drawer with flatware juddered in closing,
hiding coupons, and lyrics to songs
that frame the stanzas of every evening's lullaby,
these late days left unsung. But
I hear it. Between waves.
Unseen
like the air.
Unflinching
like the sea.

Decoration by Sean E. Sexton

Colony by Sean E. Sexton

Sean Sexton

neighborhood: Vero Beach

nominated by (Rick Campbell)

Revelation and Memory: Winter

I

Does the subject run out? Is everything over one day like a war
one never believed would end, working, living, dying here, where
you're held in the same confine—with herds of cattle: six hundred
fenced acres, only the weedy, tree-lined hedgerows barely conceal
your captivity but you're affixed by land and sky. Clouds gather
from distance by season, weather, and hour, bright, tinted, or dismal.
At some moment, levity comes to your imagining. Has it not all been
spoken of at times grandiloquently—to others in name of stewardship,
or to oneself—wresting away the impulse to harbor regret once again
in your life.

We inadvertently turned the cows on the ditchbank this morning, mis-
remembering yet perhaps knowing all the while the left-open gate;
rushed ahead to bring them back. Only grudgingly did they acquiesce.
We're out of grass—need somewhere to go—maybe this always inmost
to us. We're essentially poor—our circumstances small and never been
otherwise—bringing three hundred cows and their calves along in certain
poverty, presently fashioned upon a season that equals the stupidity of man.

II

I remember Tampa one February, stiff wind skirling off the Bay, ravaging
the State Fairgrounds. Everyone in down vests, freezing their asses off,
ducking into the main pavilion to get out of it for a moment—that tense,
quiet, concentrated air of the livestock show, class after class sequencing
hours. Then back out into that gale where speech itself—frozen—doesn't

quite catch in the ear amid wind-torn diesel clatter of the midway mixing
with aromas of candy and grease.

The Brahman Association meeting was kept till after the final class: "Get
of Sire"—whole cow families lined up—bull, dam, yearlings, and sucklings,
together like entries on a pedigree certificate as in proof of something.
The handlers, mostly farm-raised kids, lead ropes and show sticks, feverishly
stroking dewlaps and navels—all watching as they cow-towed determinedly
the circulating, dispassionate judge.

Old Boss walked the midway hunting for a vendor to sell us Cuban
sandwiches he remembered from years ago at the fair. Yet only funnel cakes,
colored ices of every radioactive hue, gewgaws, and worthless ephemera to be
found. This is the outer pocket emptying world we pass through, coming to
understand the invernal chill of Hell—not Dante's—nor from sudden loss
and derision, but the unnamable thing that can spawn and grow within your
life—malevolent cousin of hope—like a weak calf born every year and for
whatever reason, sickens and dies on your watch.

III

We conceded to hamburgers the elephant stepped on at a stand, and joined
the meeting destined to mire in pettiness--formality: the thinking-man's
whore. President, Joe Barthle at last interrupted the hour's long inanity
to say, "Gentlemen—what's your pleasure?" Old Boss had had enough,
whispered audibly, "Let's bug out of here!" and up and gone, we were soon
crossing along dusk-laden strawberry fields of Valrico and Dover, obliterat-
ing massifs of phosphate at Mulberry, Bartow's reclamations and equipment
yards and the brown, frozen expanses of prairie between podunk boiled-
peanut and fruit-stand settlements along the way.

The Kissimmee was somnolent, hyacinthine from the bridge; Blanket Bay, Peavine Trail, the Desert Inn at the crossroads, Ossawa, cut-off to Blue Cypress and Twenty-mile Bend all dissolved into a gloaming folded upon memory. How many times this trip taken before and since in my life's journey, soon melded into the days til conjuring comes from a westward glance to coloring finale or this sullen evening as the chime rings a brisk air, seeming to possess the world's breath. There will be no last glimpse of the orb, no crack in the western firmament where light has already begun to slip out of the sky into oncoming darkness.

Lola Haskins

neighborhood: Gainesville

nominated by (C.M. Clark)

The Discovery

On walking, in my seventies, down a leafy street
behind two women in their early forties who
are chatting to each other as companionably
as birds on a limb, and having thought, with
happy anticipation, ah, I'll be their age soon!
it occurs to me that I've lost my mind-- but
just then the clouds evanesce and light pours
through the oaks and ash, to form lace on
the pavement lovely enough to be sewn
into dresses, and I see that time is as
random as the patterns the sun makes on
any given day as it filters through leaves,
and as illusory as a baby being born, and
as strange as the years of our lives that
go by without returning, and as equal as
the one friend's auburn hair and the red leaf
she steps over, which the wind has abandoned
for love of her. And now, having finally
seen that the world is every minute new,
I realize that I'm only a little younger than
those women after all, and I step between
them, and we speak as we walk, and by
the time we part, each of us in her own way
has told the others how lucky she is,
to have been alive in such a beautiful place.

Originally published in *Rattle*, and included in *Homelight* (Charlotte Lit Press, 2023)

Silvia Curbelo

neighborhood: Tampa

nominated by (Lola Haskins)

Read This

In the place where sad
is a verb she holds
the window open
as if light were a book
she could live in.
Over and over
her small hands
the fragile, brimming
cup, the bluest
page. Love's tender
necessary grammar.
A flower pressed into the flesh
of a reminder. Words
twisted into feathers.
Tiny arrows. Her broken
origami bird.

This poem first appeared in *SWWIM Every Day*

Regina Dilgen

neighborhood: Delray Beach

nominated by (Judy Ireland)

Something Has Gone Terribly Wrong in the Atomic Big Time: The Movie

Saturdays as it started getting dark I watched Thriller Theater
The movies were always the same,
Something was wrong in the world, things much amiss
And the minute you realized this, you could not go back, not ever.
A man had grown to monster size, exposed to radiation.
He could only sit on the beach, wrapped in a huge cloth, waiting.
Spiders were the size of rooms, hiding in terrible caves.
These things were out there,
and now all the people in the movies knew.
Once you knew,
everything was ruined.
I watched in the rumpus room with its oversize furniture,
the garage close by
stocked with the delivery from the pretzel and soda man,
its own kind of shelter.
The grown ups
would come to say goodbye
before they left for their crowded parties.
Heavy make-up /perfume and cologne leaving fallout
They mushroomed above
Giants themselves

Originally published in *Persimmon Tree*, Winter, 2022

Richard Ryal

neighborhood: Plantation

nominated by (Lenny DellaRocca)

Lola Begins

I drift through my dark, a hull without rudder,
to follow a bell only I hear.
I can't tell you the truth, I can only mutter.

I want to pray but I barely can stutter.
Certain I'm guided, still I can't steer,
adrift through my dark, a hull without rudder.

My heart tests its sails, it races and flutters.
My mouth wants to howl, give wind to this fear
But I can't tell you the truth, I can only mutter.

My faith is too weak. Like a new calf at udder
I take it all in, then stumble back, veer
and drift through my dark, a hull without rudder.

A honey thick current bears me into utter
ruin. In my small mirror, new faces appear.
I can't tell you their truth, I can only mutter.

Then this terrible grace gives me one last shudder
and passes, familiar pains return with their sear.
I drift through my dark, a hull without rudder.
I can't tell you the truth, I can only mutter.

Originally published in *Notre Dame Review* Issue No. 55, Summer/Winter 2023

Little Haiti by Erik Ebright

Oscar Fuentes / The Biscayne Poet

neighborhood: Miami

---

nominated by (Nicole Tallman)

Little Haiti (Bonswa Mesye O)
(part of a new animated film, and original music has been composed
by Sydney Guillaume)

I walk my dog Max every evening after work. I live off Biscayne Boulevard
and 64th Street.

We cross Biscayne and Max leads me all the way to the heart of Little Haiti,
the Cultural Center on 54th street.

On our way there I swear we can smell the aroma of all the different types of
dinners being cooked.

The scent is so rich and colorful.

There are four houses where the families actually set their dinners out on
their patios.

Their dogs have even stopped barking at us because we've become familiar to
them.
Yesterday we actually started waving hello.
We usually turn right back around after we arrive at the Little Haiti
Cultural Center.
That's when our walk gets interesting.

By the time we start to cross the neighborhood, we can smell coffee in the
wind mixed with a touch of cigar smoke.

Two of the houses that have dinner under the stars always bring out their

conga drums and bongos while they sip on their coffee.
We walk by slowly and listen to them sing together softly, in Creole.

Max usually speeds up his walk after we pass the two music houses and he
slows down at the boulevard.

The motels with their neon lights flickering. The billboard of the
Coppertone girl with the pooch in the distance.

Everyone stops on red. Max pulls and we cross the street. They all drive on
green.
Max pulls me east all the way down to Biscayne Bay.

We stop right by the water. We both sigh. I mean, how could we not be
influenced by this.

M.B. McLatchey

neighborhood: New Smyrna Beach

nominated by (Sarah Carey)

Rate My Professor: A Rebuttal

Do not take. She makes you
talk no matter where you sit.

I greeted you at the door, another mother's
child delivered. You looked away as if a lamb
had been slain. Your early sounds parsed, seeds
seeking ground – then whole thoughts crowned.

Ridiculous grader. She actually reads
your work instead of the deserved A.

So hard to put a score on this – this wrestling with
your age. Rubrics hold out such promise – then fold,
fade. Instead of systems: a new thought, like a starling
transporting a golden bough, was what we praised.

I didn't come here to read ancient epics, poems, plays.
Remind me again how this gets an engineer employed?

Leaving Troy, Odysseus had one thing – Ithaca – in mind.
The gods gave him their scales: slay the proud boy in you
and die a king regaled. A cyclops, sirens, a bard spared among
suitors to sing your tale. All of them pleading: *Set sail. Set sail.*

Originally published in *Sky Island Journal, Issue #23*, Winter 2023

Untitled by Christina Nwabugo

Susannah W. Simpson

neighborhood: West Palm Beach

---

nominated by (Regina Dilgen)

Tao

The Eight-Fold Path is Saturn's glittering rings. The Eight-Fold Path unveils
a beginner's guide through the Nine Palaces, caverns filled with treasure. The
Eight-fold path is silent steps, padded feet, Hemingway's many toed cats.
It charts Heaven's Seven Domes inlaid with a thousand jeweled suns. It is
a Merlin crystal, six-sided clarity. The Eight- fold path is our human form.
Five-points. Starfish, clinging to vast ocean bottoms. The Eight-fold path is
a compass through our Western tangled brush, Southern moist summers,
Eastern shores, and Northern deep-sky lakes. It is the Five elements, and
exact stripe count of a zebra's pelt. The Eight-fold path is Scottish meadow
thistle, armored plates on armadillo pups, soft owlet feathers the Eight-fold
path is to circle back.

Kris Thurston

neighborhood: Boynton Beach

---

nominated by (Susannah W. Simpson)

What They Don't Tell You about Organ Donation

Hearts are the hardest.
They have to stop completely
before they can make their chilly trip
in their white and red coolers
to nestle in a new body.
Kidneys, liver, other organs also lose
their pink perfusion past
a down-to-the-second-ninety-minute window.

 To be an organ donor,
our son, only 32 years old,
has to pass this one last test.

And Ben keeps breathing.

And the window shuts.
The transplant team leaves.
The gentle technician watching his monitors
turns them off.
We follow the stretcher down a dark hallway,
in and out of the elevator,
back to the ICU.

And Ben keeps breathing.

His doctor tells us this could continue
for minutes, hours, weeks--
while Ben lies still--
looking as if he might, at any moment, turn,
open his eyes,
and whisper, *let's go home.*

Peter Meinke

neighborhood: St. Petersburg

nominated by (M.B. McLatchey)

The Last Holiday

. . . all day under the sun with hoe and hose
taking advantage of the holiday to whip
his garden into shape which he is out of
so when it's time to watch the fireworks

he begs off *Poor old dad* closing
his door that evening *losing it missing*
the show   But behind his shut lids shimmer
crinkled streamers of Boston fern

sparklers of campanula and carnation
daisy pinwheels and ginger flares:
a pyrotechnical dandelion parachutes
on the black wind and high above them all

spraying like a burst star
a perfect *Rosa multiflora*
its petals dissolving in the patriotic dark
like pink aspirin . . .

Apalachicola 3 by Lenny DellaRocca

Llewellyn McKernan

neighborhood: Daytona Beach

nominated by (Ellen Neilsen)

An Unknown Angel

spikes the dice to even the odds, changes the face
of the woodland fog, dictates the shape of absence,
the shadow at noon, if there were one.

She's the seven white waves that give way to the
sea, the speed that breaks the sound barrier, the
muscles that flex the chaos of your dreams, your

face most like hers when you turn the lonely crowd
of your past into a present your mother unwraps
for Christmas. Her wings bloom from one nudge,

a thousand red feathers filling earth and sky with a
bright language, one written in air, on leaf, between
every grain the earthworm turns, but most of all

in what you grasp when you stumble and fall,
slipping down the steps of a fault into the dark of
the underworld: here angel-shine shrinks to one

glowing thread you pull through the needle of
desire, sewing up the cold, wet, richly torqued
inscrutable depths. You grow light, inscribing

on black walls with invisible chalk the meaning
of your life. Turning three times—once for faith,
once for hope, once for love itself—you walk in

your own shoes as you climb back up through a
stone crevice, your breath a bellow pumping the
red-hot valves of your heart, its alphabet of blood.

Blaise Allen

neighborhood: Deerfield Beach

nominated by (Lenny DellaRocca)

Over The Moon

I'm finished with late night epiphanies.
I've had enough of you insisting
you're a "New Moon," when you
disappear for days and show up with
the same dark side you always had.

Notorious, lothario moon, I know you
cavort with other women, wink
and flirt when I turn my back.
I realize you're just too high
and mighty to be faithful to one.

I know all your aliases: Deer moon,
Singing moon, Hunter moon, Harvest moon.
I'm squashed by your pumpkin heaviness.
You really are a Snake moon!

I'm done with moon metaphors:
You thrown from a potters wheel
and fired white,
You hooked like a flounder,
You as a communion wafer,
You carnal crazy-maker
exposing your alabaster breast.

I'll have no more of your Moonpies
or crescent moons sautéed with cloud
mushrooms. I'm bored lying under you.
I'm done with your cheesy songs.
I'm through being eclipsed by your glow.
How long must one wait to see you again?
I'm done pining for you! You're too full of yourself.
I'm no longer moon drunk, or starry-eyed,
I'll never touch a drop of Moonshine again.

Brendan Walsh

neighborhood: Hollywood

nominated by (Gregg Shapiro)

cedar key

roseate spoonbills hotpink in the live oak
across the saltpond fly out with the tides
so pronounced such flamboyant high-low
swings the fish jump constantly towards sun
the noseeums eat-us-up tonight as we dismantle
clams our fingers oiled and garlicked
everything must feed

the dolphins in the bay who barely
touch our kayak with their cartoonish snouts
hunt fish differently than other dolphins
they've constructed distinct divisions of labor
to secure meals for every mouth
this is their culture this is who they are
we forget that culture is a human word

for universal animal behavior like how the spoonbills
on cedar key prefer some small marsh minnows
unavailable further west or south
or how i've cooked this steak for us and you knew
the farmer maybe even knew the cow we name
every bite of food we name birds and forget kinds of fish
except the few we like to eat

imagine shellmound just east of here without
thousands of years of discarded shells
left by the killed-off indigenous people
their civilization defined by clam and oyster
and we know nothing of what they called themselves

or who they loved and now white people come
to study their trash and theorize about extinction

what will we leave behind in this place
not bottles or plastic bags not these scraps
which are trucked off-island to a regional landfill
how quiet it will be once we're gone oh thank god
this noiseless world these miles of tidal swamp
fishjump and birdhonk an unnamed song
the gulf growing rich with emptiness

Originally published in *Sidereal Magazine*

Spanish Moss Sunset by Jeff Ronci

Flamingo, Everglades National Park, Florida

Peter Hargitai

neighborhood: Gulfport

nominated by (Howard Camner)

Opening at Town Shores

From a drone
The man-made waterways
Spread out their fingers
A sailboat sputters
Past humdrum condominiums
Toward the mouth
Of Boca Ciega Bay
The old Mercury puffs
A few thick clouds
Before it stalls

Then a lull

The timing near perfect:
The wind billows the sails
Full sail ahead
The ageless current
That drives the air
That stirs the water
And moves the hull
Toward the sea moves me
And causes my fingers
To move across the page

The drone zooms in
To showcase the pool
Jutting into a widening channel
The area is deserted
Except for an old man

Near the pool's edge
Regally robed and safari helmeted
Sitting and writing
In the cage of his
Aluminum walker

It is summer in Florida

He interrupts himself
To look around
Then goes back to recording
The secret life of insects and plants

Zoom in closer:
I am that man

I open myself to the silence
There's enough of it here
To hear the tiniest of wings
Gone is the drone above
And the one taking wing
From MacDill Air Base

It is the sound of a frail creature
Swollen with pollen
Toiling to hold itself up
In the nothingness of air
Waiting with grace
For the fall

The inevitable splash

In that same instant
Sun sparklers trawl their nets
Across the surface
To catch this quiet

How could I have missed it?
Something sacred was about to land

Swimmers invade the pool
Instead of swimming they stand
In the water or move a limb
Talk of tai chi and yoga
And cancer and catheters
A father with Alzheimer's
A neighbor's lingering terminal illness
A death

For a few seconds all is quiet
Maybe too quiet
The air begins to cloy
With baby oil and iodine
A professor whose gray hair is braided
Announces that the spirit
Must be grounded in light
Another interrupts her
About The Power of Now
Soon all is aflutter
The sounds distant and nonsensical
As the chirping of birds

What they leave behind
Is stillness so maddening
The shrill lawnmower
Is welcome noise

Stillness then
Is not the absence of sound
And loveliness not always a flower
Unless I see it for the first time
How the filaments in the center
Thinner than paper

Aspire upward
Opening
Never preening
And when its time has come
A petal does not mind drying
Never minds
Falling

Under the eyes
Of a mechanical owl
And barrier fishing lines
Two Florida sparrows land
To gulp water
Splash one another
And spur the moment to frolic
One flies away
The other looks on
The slight wings beating water
To drown its sorrow
Before it too flies off
In the same direction

Stillness is not
Always the lack of motion
The birds were not nervous
When they gave themselves
Over to doing what they do
They have flown beyond artificial nets
Even ceremonial doves
Defy formation without
Fretting about falling
Or bettering their last
Audition

On the Tiki hut
A palm frond loses its footing

The vertical drop
Fans into a swan dive
Still it misses the water
And scrapes along the pool's edge
Waiting to be airborne again

In the shadow
Of a sundial
A caterpillar plant comes to life
Breakdancing to a sudden gust
The stem shivers and little hairs
Thin and fall

Into transparence
In the whitening sun
Each floats on air
To its own rhythm
Its own
Stylized breaking crawl

The mower cuts all that lands
In its path into finer filigree
To be airlifted or sprayed
Into green water
And carried out colorless
As they reach the sea
They are as much a part of the great
Current as the dancing seahorse
The feather star
Or the rainbow anemone
What was dander in the grass
Is now a great spirit
More brilliant in its sheerness
Than the oleander

The pool light comes on underwater

I watch the lightshow on the bottom
Lace curtains dance into and out of focus
And shudder at the slightest touch
A single breath from me sets off ripples
Changing the mesh of an entire universe
Each pattern more intricate than the last
As sound waves translate
Into shape-shifting
Fractals of light
I keep blowing on the surface
Mesmerized by zebras crawling
Down my leg
The shifting lines continue to drill
Their spiraling illusions
Right through the concrete
To the underside of life
All I do is to poke a finger
In the water and—voila!
A diaphanous mandala
Alive and billowing
Spreads out and downward
And starts to gel
In the viscous slow motion
Of a lava lamp overflowing
To an underground river
And an endless formless
Waxen ocean

The submarine light
Insinuates itself through
The murky green of night vision
Into the very treacle of the sea
And what unfolds before the eye
Is an undulating breathing
Undiscovered yet familiar
—opening—

Forming and reforming
In fleeting time-lapse
Corals becoming reefs becoming
An island
The runway of the landing

As I tread way
Into the secret life of the jungle
Leaves waver
Dry and yellow
Into haystacks of old Europe
Changing in shape and color
Into towers of Cholla cactuses
Teepee huts crowned with
The feathers of raised spirits

Images of burial mounds
Subterranean pyramids
Glowing embers red and volcanic
Burst and spatter
Every edifice
Cornice and porous
Surface of concrete jungle
With a riotous magma of color
Melting and molding
Every molecule
Into sacred geometry

Gecko gargoyles mechanical owls
A razor-sharp sunburst
Appear in Day-Glo colors
To scare off buzzards
Unwanted solicitors
And all other bloodsuckers
That impersonate time

From the humble Kenmore
To Embassy row
Condominiums raise
Their sacred totems
To the beat of Tocobaga drums
An ancient wind instrument
Billows the sails
And makes the fingers of water tremble

Artists bricklayers dragon slayers
Sailors and whistling minstrels
Woman warriors
Weary from battles for their
Own secret heart
Every grain of sand
Blown here from distant shores
Every brush and crush of petal
Filament of flower sundial and owl
An animate and timeless
Sacrament of grace

From *Opening at Town Shores* (YellowJacket Press, 2019). Copyright © 2019 Peter Hargitai. Used with permission of the author.

Jonathan Rose

neighborhood: Miami Beach

nominated by (Peter Hargitai)

Lettered

Puritan New England' Hester Prynne
In her day, wore an "A" for unspeakable sin.
Now with sex extramarital, kinky, and group,
The fashion would be to wear alphabet soup.

first published in *South Florida Poetry Review*

Indecisive

Hamlet, the Dane,
Was a royal pain.
It would not have meant a jot to me
Had he determined "not to be."

for published in *Poetic Justice*

Vested

Thomas Howard, alias Jesse James,
Was a businessman, despite contrary claims;
Bullish on banks for most financial gains,
He was the first to speculate with trains.

first published in *Rhyme Time*

Unforeseen

William Sidney Porter
Was a clever retorter;

Through his briefest tale you'd go twisting and bending
To be stunned with a wonderful O. Henry ending.

Originally published in *Writer's Info*

Lost

Amelia Earhart, renowned flier,
Prided herself as a "do-or-dier;"
We know her position when she last flew,
But that was one time she did not "do."

Originally published in *Rhyme Time*

Deceptive

Poet-theologian John Donne
Ostensibly would accede to no fun,
But, I have it on reliable account,
Themes for his sermons came while on the mount.

Originally published in *South Florida Poetry Review*

Apalachicola 2 by Lenny DellaRocca

James Kimbrell

neighborhood: Tallahassee

nominated by (Steve Kronen)

Green Ouija

If my parents left anything unsaid, they kept it to themselves
before stepping into that breeze that blows backwards,
into that boat that rows beyond passage. If I could hear,
if I could reach their nearest syllable, then I would know

I have assumed the body of the Mississippi sandhill crane
I've always wanted to be. If my sisters could fly beside me,
we'd count the teardrop sandbars down the Chickasawhay,
tipping our gray feathers. This is just to say, if the dead

could send a message, it might be written in the cursive
of bees hovering above my uncut grass. If I could read
their flight, I wouldn't need to be satisfied with missing

my father. These are the conditions of the cosmos
and gravity, from which I cannot budge. Meanwhile, airplanes
look like boats motoring overhead, the sky is that deep.

Originally published in *Grass Routes*, 2021 and in James's manuscript, *The Law of Truly Large Numbers*

David Kirby

neighborhood: Tallahassee

---

nominated by (Lenny DellaRocca)

Taking It Home to Jerome

In Baton Rouge, there was a DJ on the soul station who was
always urging his listeners to "take it on home to Jerome."

No one knew who Jerome was. And nobody cared. So it
didn't matter. I was, what, ten, twelve? I didn't have anything

to take home to anyone. Parents and teachers told us that all
we needed to do in this world were three things: be happy,

do good, and find work that fulfills you. But I also wanted
to learn that trick where you grab your left ankle in your

right hand and then jump through with your other leg.
Everything else was to come, everything about love:

the sadness of it, knowing it can't last, that all lives must end,
all hearts are broken. Sometimes when I'm writing a poem,

I feel as though I'm operating that crusher that turns
a full-size car into a metal cube the size of a suitcase.

At other times, I'm just a secretary: the world has so much
to say, and I'm writing it down. This great tenderness.

Landis Grenville

neighborhood: Tallahassee

nominated by (David Kirby)

45 Union Line to Presidio

When the child was a child,
It didn't know it was a child.

Sometimes the sky can be this close, dawn weighing across
roofs and in the net of trolley lines, a city asleep
under the table of the world, but for this slight of hand
as night's linens strip to blue. And I have given up on being
a saved woman. I want this city and its lively ossuary.
Just the worship of a bus on time and in the right direction.
Heading along into the accident of my life as it arrives
and retreats along the fine thread of the hour. And looking out,
why here and not there? One purple flower outside the window.
Two aspirin for the headache I've had all night. Sometimes
the world confiding itself behind the blare of the sun
is too much to hear all at once! It says, *turn away*, and I do.
And why not? Earth is still a beautiful place to die. Once,
my mother sewed white feathers to cardboard and dressed us
in the gauze of flight and the smack of pearls as we landed.
It is true I do not want to die. Though nor do I want to be
an orchard governed, paradise remedied of the ordinary I.
Odd to say the world is as old as man though the dirt is older.
In the scalpeled breeze of the bus departing, I stumble
through the park already crowded by the plectra of voices.
This simple stage—grass and asphalt, a child's pink giraffe--
all arriving out of nothing. Teenagers interrupt the field, huddling
in the grass to sip from a single gas station cup. The nannies
on the benches, lit in morning, slip into small laughter. Alone,
I press into the stillness of a concrete wall edging along the grass.
The light ardent through my eyes shut. No one is noticing
the baby boy, down on his knees in the center of the playground,
his eyes pinning that fugitive sky. Grace is the body arriving
in present tense. I am only saying, *not yet, not yet.*

Abel Folgar

neighborhood: Miami

---

nominated by (Lúcia Leão)

Lazarus

Lazarus, Lazarus, frail Lazarus, entombed and forgotten
     to the musky cold of Israelite cave.
Green-skinned Lazarus, sweet friend absconded and risen again
     —the original comeback kid--
more return from the fists than modern pugilists.
     You'd never squander wealth,
get your prick diseased, pug Lazarus, the four-day boy;
     no, you lived too concerned
for lonely Mary and Martha and the wandering eyes of friends.
     Southpaw Lazarus, lovable Lazarus,
you never took to their trusting friendship in Jesus
     during those troubled Aramaic times.
Good son Lazarus, always on guard, the sickness took you by surprise,
     divinely deliberate and fast;
an up-and-comer's lightning one-two, no rest and one-two again--
     never gave you a chance
to counter, parry, work the damn ropes, whittle down their stamina.
     He took his time,
though they begged and begged; doubting Lazarus, human Lazarus,
     body taut and cold,
your sneaking suspicions that the special friend had more
     than parables to feed the girls;
barbaric retribution into the bonds of slavery through reanimation.
     Patient Lazarus, calculating Lazarus;
take your time, your kin come first, walk the ring, circle in--
     as the new day's light hits your eyes
you think through the jab's haze, believe and never die he said?
     Shit, I think I'll punch him first.

Lúcia Leão

neighborhood: Boca Raton

nominated by (Jennifer Litt)

Yellowed Summers

In Florida

In the kitchen, months of January,
months of December enter my Julys.
A pineapple rings home.

A disposition of oranges
nests among the ferns as they awaken,
yawning as the green dew
dries up the night.

Lightning divided the afternoon yesterday.

A white plate in the sink shows
residues of skin.

Iguana by Alvaro Gutierrez

Jennifer Litt

neighborhood: Fort Lauderdale

nominated by (Susan Williamson)

March

I'd like to revise the weather proverb to this—*March
comes in like a twice-thawed iguana & out like a Key deer*;
I'd like to rewrite Act 3, Scene 1 of Shakespeare's *Julius
Caesar*, so Caesar eats himself to death on Little Caesar's
Italian Sausage Pizza, because March is not about murder,
but about suicide; I'd like to say to every Pisces embellisher
of truth — *the fault is in your stars & the lies you tell yourself.*
I'd like to clear the sidewalks of St. Patrick's Day drunks
lying in their puke after the parade, give them the evil ides.
Uber me to a sanctuary where the healer exorcises green
iguanas digging burrows inside of me, wreaking havoc
on my infrastructure & infecting me with lethargy. I'd
like to protect my solitude, as the nearly extinct Key
deer found its niche on the endangered species list.

Yaddyra Peralta

neighborhood: Miami

nominated by (Jennifer Litt)

Even at the Masonic Temple Near the Miami River, I Think of Hialeah

It grazes the clouds, but not like a skyscraper high above
a city. This pavilion's crowd is invisible. Voices long dead
whisper past the Doric columns, elephantine and marvelous.
They scuttle about the vaulted hallways to find a cleft
through which to rise up toward the roof, ziggurat topped
by a cupola resembling an ancient priest's temple,
fortified as if to protect against enemies, high-placed
as if to avoid rising waters. What danger
from this River then, so short and peripheral?

Sometimes I am just a girl, still in Hialeah, whose name
means pretty prairie or high prairie depending on who you ask.
That jury-rigged city, strip malls and molding houses canal-side.
The waters near there meander, carry our hum like overladen cargo.
In Miami, we are all little girls from Hialeah,
excavating potholed pavement for the past, so
recent, and so bewildering. If the temple lifts our old song
of limestone, marl, and muck, speaks our new tongue
of steel and glass, then our disembodied din aims high
for sky-bound transmission to the near-atmosphere,
older than Miami, as everything but the future is.

Susan R. Williamson

neighborhood: Boca Raton

---

nominated by (Lenny DellaRocca)

Trimming The Robellini Palm Tree in Front of My Condo

I never notice I need to bring out the clippers until one day it rains
and a palm frond slaps me in the face as I try to cross into the entrance
to my front doorway. It's not a grand residence, our Florida condo.

When we arranged for landscaping out front, I chose this tree. It was
a lot younger, three separate trunks growing together, knee high because
I thought my husband would like that and he did.

Symbols of Florida at the doorway, swaying in the breeze. Palms out front
would be a miniature nod to Palm Beach, the grand avenues or the public
gardens and guarded entrances to private communities, their Royal Palms

towering above gates. As I reach up with the clippers, I try to avoid
the spines, sharp and visible near the base of the branch. I never knew
they were there until the first time I was stabbed.

Until the light changed I couldn't see what hit me. Not a spider or a mosquito
but a palm thorn, heavy like a rug needle and sharp. I've learned a thing or
two about this palm as it now stands alone.

It's grown taller than the railing of the stairs to the apartment above.
Squirrels like to take the thatch for their nests by stripping the bark,
stealing what's left after a frond is cut before it spikes the next frond.

It's alone now, the two others that lived with it are gone. Squirrel damage,
or maybe this one was the strongest. I've had it for just about fifteen
years now. I can see it from my desk, through the window.

A solo act, withstanding the sieges of the squirrels, hurricane winds,
the bluejay that comes to hide a peanut, wedging it between the bark,
the little anole lizards that rest there, red throats puffing out to attract

mosquitoes and gnats. The black snake curled at its base, the Cuban Anole,
foot-long green lizard with the yellow and red stripe under its eyes.
Every year around this time, I trim it back hard, only a tuft of fronds left

at the top. In this hurricane season the branches are so tall and lush they
whip around in the wind and throw water on my window. Sometimes I think
it's my husband about to come through the door. But it's just the palm tree,

throwing its weight around with the waving green fronds. Standing
out there alone now, like me. Nobody is in the other room, or coming home
later. It will have to weather more storms alone. And so will I.

Becka Mara McKay

neighborhood: Delray Beach

nominated by (Lúcia Leão)

Leviticus as Punchline for a Bad Joke

The president walked into history
like a battery of gnats swarming summer's

lost wine. Each commandment you unearth—
hued in chalcedony and anthracite,

divided with camels and cattle—
offers further fuel for the argument

with God: Did He mean, in the end, to punish
us or protect us? Are we experiment

or intention? The president was disgorged
into history, bad meat in a linen napkin.

Some of us gave up. Some of us said
let the consecrated field be the home he cannot

destroy. Maybe everything that refuses
God's abstraction becomes a kind of mutation,

like the thought that warps and splits on its way
to the word. The president met history

dressed in suit and tie but would not shake hands.
Let the consecrated field remain in the grip

of the gleaners, who crouch at the edges
and wait, sheaving their needs against darkness.

Untitled by Robert Kso

Laurie Kuntz

neighborhood: West Palm Beach

nominated by (Lúcia Leão)

Anhinga Drying Her Wings

Where has she flown
for the need to stop
on a lily pad and spread
wet tipped wings
under the ebb of day?

What venture caused
her to dive into this lagoon
black with its endless bottom?

Who are we, passersby,
to disturb her stance
on reeds fragile to sight
and thought of these steps
we both make on sandy roads?

Under waning suns
winged and footed journeys
are beginning anew
and ending, marked
with the coming
of first snow and last rose.

Originally published in *Poetry Breakfast*

Cicadas by Francesco Ungaro

Stacie M. Kiner

neighborhood: Hypoluxo

nominated by (Patricia Whiting)

Bethesda

Cicadas are genetically programmed
to emerge from hibernation
every 17 years. —Newsweek

Has it been 17 years
since we sat on the deck
of a restaurant in Bethesda,
eating Maryland blue crabs
and drinking beer?

We spoke the language
of wind -
palm and banana leaves,
thinking that made a difference;

but even wind
needs a place
to stay.

I remember
how long ago it was
because of the cicadas'
return.

There were so many of them -
trillions emerge
in a synchronous way...
a strong survival strategy.

When we tried to outrun them,
The Metro
to Dupont Circle -
they made a home
in your hair.

Was that our strategy -
running up steps
emerging into something
we could
never outrun?

Telling ourselves we can
move on from loss
is rain held
in a gray sky
that never falls.

Now, we're the town
with no name,
no post office –
a commemorative plaque
on a scenic highway,
where a photograph
hangs on a rusting hook
on a porch

with one lamp
left on.

David Eileen

neighborhood: Fort Lauderdale

---

nominated by (Becka Mara McKay)

This is a Collection of

what's good for the goose is good for the deeply personal poem / I'm trying to lose five or ten deeply personal poems / deeply personal poems are the original superfood / doctors hate this one weird deeply personal poem / it's ten o'clock on a Saturday night do you know where your deeply personal poem is / deeply personal poems are the world's largest underground network of caves / so cold / limestone and dark / many deeply personal poems make light work / that's what my dad always said / deeply personal poems are a great source of vitamin D / a magician never reveals their deeply personal poems / but what's in those sleeves / are you fucking deeply personal poems or nah / the Wi-Fi password is deeply personal poems / have you tried turning them off and on again / I brought you into this deeply personal poem and I can take you right back out again/ we'll cross that deeply personal poem when we come to it / do you think we'll live to see the end of deeply personal poems in our lifetime / deeply personal poems are clocking in and out of work / it is time theft / KILL deeply BURN personal FUCK poems/ mirror mirror on the wall who is the most deeply personal poem / Keeping Up With The deeply personal poems / a friend in need is a friend in deeply personal poems / did you hear they're building a new deeply personal poem / downtown / with a patio / they're going to have bottomless deeply personal poems with Sunday brunch / legalize deeply personal poems / the best time to plant a deeply personal poem is twenty years ago / the second best time is today / hallelujah it's raining deeply personal poems / the bodies are everywhere / please and deeply personal poems are the magic words / deeply personal poems are a bold choice like a smoky eye / or a bright lip / or a tight skirt / hold me closer deeply personal poems / deeply personal poems were just arrested in connection to a homicide / police say the suspect was under the influence of deeply personal poems / some of my best friends are deeply personal poems / but I keep asking /where they are really from

Originally published in *Alien Magazine* and in *Best of the Net 2020*, an anthology by Sundress Publications

Zoraida "Ziggy" Pastor

neighborhood: Miami

nominated by (Lenny DellaRocca)

Be Like Mary Oliver

In the early morning,

before the ibis shakes herself from her sleep
in the trees,
before the sun wakes up.

You can see her:
Square jaw, thick glasses,
nicotine-stained skin,

walking this forest,
always with a pencil in hand,

a cigarette on her lips,

her notebook abuzz

with her words.

Her coat tattered by branches of
so many trees.

She follows a snail then climbs a tree.

She sees two hummingbirds

talking to each other,

listening to each other's song.

One flies away.

The tree shudders alive

with its colors.

She climbs down,

heads to the marsh,

to find mussels

sleeping on the side of a
barnacle.

She thanks the mussel for its life,

that she now has breakfast.

She returns home.

Cleans and prepares the mussels.
She eats and begins to type.

Her white page waiting all morning.

Ismael Santos

neighborhood: Miami

---

nominated by (Ziggy Pastor)

I used to dream about Love

I used to dream about Love. I sighed, like Percy Bysshe
Shelley, Brooding on snowy mountaintops, ever the Romantic

I pined and pined and prayed and cried,
Waiting for someone, for Love to come and recognize me, me,
me. That did not work.
It never does.

I wrote poems, texts, letters, and sent them off, like ravens
Flying through the Gothic night, like carrier pigeons with little letters

Tied to their feet. It did not lead me anywhere, except for the
ability To write about such things. Went on dates, and didn't say a
word/ Didn't get dates and pondered what was I missing out on/
Years passed,
Still, I dreamed, and wrote, and wanted to express my own insatiable soul.

I threw all I had into what I thought you were, Love. The dream of Love
Was soon replaced by Reality.

I tried to live and accept it,
But the Old Ways are deeply rooted, and hard to let go of. SO, I myself
    drifted
apart, finding myself disconnected, detached, and wholly alone.

I didn't want Love.
Imagining the days of more dates, of more Tinder swipes, of more random
bar, and life, connections. Hopping from one hope
to the next. And knowing the end result.

the end result:

Sleep, bathroom, repeat.

The days passed.
I forgot about Love.
Love seemed like a squatter in a condemned building, doomed to be
gone Any moment, any second.
Like a distant memory of a trip, like a day spent with
insomnia. I did not, would not, could not believe in it,
anymore.
But, time passes, as it always does, and something strange
happened: Love, you came back. But just a little differently.

Instead of the man screaming love and waving around
flowers to any and all who would ever look upon him,
the Love became the man
scattering the flowers around him,
and saying hi to the bees, their pollination
another cycle of the life.

Now, love seemed like a familiar neighbor.
I am unafraid to say that I, too, feel love, and love, in return.

The Brooding Romantic on the Snowy Cliffs of Dover
Resides more in these words.

The days go by quickly and fuller, somehow. Love is just love to me,
now. No more madness/And yet,

I still wonder.

Apalachicola 1 by Lenny DellaRocca

Jeff Santosuosso

neighborhood: Miami

nominated by (Lenny DellaRocca)

Railyard Just West of Kansas City

The railyard throws out its chest, stretches its shoulders.
The Earth below bursts with track,
swells with wheels, fat with freight,
forms a delta, an enormous steel cattle drive.
I see the cars of the nation,
cars beside cars beside cars beside cars.

Beneath me, Kansas City.
Parked freight awaits
arrival and delivery,
promises kept by the carload,
futures secured with linkages and couplings,
engines and smoke, lurches and whistles,
choked by tonnage that yields to
the raw power of coal,
like the Earth's exhalations
blowing boulders across a continent.

I am certain of stock pilers,
lifting and heaving, sweating
in winter, breath
bellowing work into daylight
of this great congestion, this standing-room-only
stadium of goods, of hardware, livestock,
grains, coal and parcels,
this economy bursting like cotton bolls
blinding whiteness across the Delta.

Amaryllis by Dillon Pena

Laura Sobbott Ross

neighborhood: Mount Dora

---

nominated by (Jeff Santosuosso)

Amaryllis

We readied the bulbs in the days before
the baby arrived. Full solstice moon
nudging what was curled inside its own
winter sleep; every bulb, nested & rooting.
Miraculous, the way green startled
out, ribboned toward the light--
light that was a new dominion
lording across a tracery of capillaries,
eyelashes, flutter of breath,
the fusing of the soft crown of bone.
I'm talking about the baby,
of course, whose wails shuddered open
from her newly dredged lungs, while amaryllis
pushed and pushed its flame points skyward
till they fell over on their new, floppy necks
into the full-throated red of bell-shaped blossoms.

Originally published in *National Poetry Review*

Jim Steele

neighborhood: Howie-in-the Hills

nominated by (Laura Sobbott Ross)

Sweet Silence

The mountain we see from a distance changes when we
gaze up from its base. There is beauty that is meant to
be enjoyed from a distance—it's why we can't stand
within our own horizon.

She sat on the right side of same park bench everyday,
on her lunch break. She rarely ate though, choosing to
read instead, mostly the classics—F. Scott, Jane,
and Ernest. For a couple months, I always sat on the other
end of the same bench, also reading, while stealing
glances in muted fascination. I never spoke to her.
Our tilted-head-hello's was our only conversation.

Then one day she arrived and I was sitting on the opposite
end of the bench— her end. She paused for a moment and
I looked up. She dipped her head hello and seated herself on
the left side. On the third day of our new locations, she
turned to me from her end of the bench and spoke up,
"I've been wondering why you switched ends. You always
sat here and then suddenly over there."
She half-smiled, in brightened curiosity.
After a few moments, I replied: "It may sound silly but
I noticed that if I sit here, your shadow falls across me
and I think it's romantic."
Her eyes widened, her mouth opened slightly— "Oh, I love that."
I smiled sadly and stood, "I did too."
I nodded my head goodbye and walked away,
I never returned to our bench. I never saw her again.

No friendship could measure up to what I had imagined
in that sweet, full silence. The romantic in me had no desire
to travel toward her, knowing the wonder I'd imagined
would only change.
She was part of my horizon. Nothing more.

Sharlyn Page

neighborhood: Mount Dora

---

nominated by (Jim Steele)

The Ripening

When early from the infinite, I
chose the twig that touched the sky

Hearkened to a sound first heard
from topmost leaf, susurrant word,

It was the sky-tolled call of home,
and recognition rustled down the bone.

Then my body in a seeding race
became Earth's transient spawning place,

Life called out, hoarse from earth,
the rounded body insisted birth,

As suckling newborns, wet and red,
force surrender to this self-made bed.

Here below are voiceless gardens,
seedlings faint for thirst,

I rise to bring the water,
stoop to raise the earth.

Granted a god inchoate to hold,
mute till touch is voice,

I learn the need to feed at root,
oblique to choice.

Jesse Millner

neighborhood: Estero

nominated by (Michael Hettich)

Affirmation

for Joseph Kromelis, the Walking Man

For decades, Joseph Kromelis walked alone along the city's busy downtown streets, mile after mile, regardless of the season. Tall and lean, with a bushy mustache and flamboyant hair, the urbane, sharply dressed stranger fascinated his fellow pedestrians and Loop workers. He was rarely seen talking to other people in the crowd, adding to his mystery. -Chicago Tribune, June 11th, 2023.

The homeless man I saw often in downtown Chicago all through the 1980s,
wanders down Wacker Drive this Saturday in August.

Now it's the 21st century, and yes, he still has drooping mustache, a chiseled face,
but the long hair has grayed, and his waist has shrunk to bone.

He wears old clothes and he's always walking.
Yes, that's how I remember him and how I see him now,

as my wife and I walk south on Wabash,
where the Trump Tower has long replaced the old Sun-Times

black, aircraft carrier on the Chicago River. I whisper
to my wife, try to explain the shock

of seeing this ancient figure, almost like a Chinese
poet resurrected from the mist, how strange

this old memory pasted over the new city,
bones emerging from the tired flesh.

Yes, we are both older, the wandering man and I.
Yes, I used to drive a bus in the city,

and he crossed against the traffic lights,
ignoring those flashing signals of "yes" and "no."

And sometimes his jaywalking pissed me off
as he held up my right turn on to Michigan Avenue,

but now that anger seems less than petty,
and now I'm seeing the true shape of this city,

this world, this life with all its roaring emptiness.
For hundreds of years, old poets wandered

the cold of withered landscapes that shivered
in the shade of western mountains.

For hundreds of years they crapped in the fields
and tried to capture the still beauty

of that one cloud above, shaped like the horse
they knew in childhood.

Yes, that horse, the one who so mightily
trembled when given the apple.

Yes, it's always good to bring horses
into poems, whether they come from the sky

or from memory, or from some tattered
weaving of sky and yesterday.

Yes, I see my grandfather's horse, a brown
figure in a sea of green tobacco leaves,

Billy Buck sweats in the hot Virginia sun,
pulls a sled filled with the dusky harvest.

Each bead of perspiration is a "yes."
The white diamond on his forehead

affirms every motion of his brown body.
I can still hear the pounding hooves,

fifty-years later, five decades into my continental
drifting from South to West, to Chicago,

and finally to this morning in Florida,
and yes, it's hot, and yes, the summer

flowers glow orange, red, and yellow,
and yes, the cloud factory is simmering

deep in the Everglades, and yes, this summer
afternoon will be filled with rain and lightning,

and yes, I will gather every storm memory up
into my arms, and yes, I will love

those days that have circled, then fallen into the ring
of night. And yes, I will be more humble

as I look into the faces of trees and animals,
into the wet beauty of this living world,

waxy tangerine, gleaming slash pine, stout mango,
even a blessed pineapple rising from its spiny green throne.

Originally published in Jesse's chapbook *My Grandfather Singing* (Yellowjacket Press, 2009).

Apalachicola 5 by Lenny DellaRocca

Michael Mackin O'Mara

neighborhood: West Palm Beach

nominated by (Stephen Gibson)

a poem is an exorcism from the inside out
a death threat, an oracle, a billboard of fresh air,
news from the front,

a poem is a writ of habeas corpus, a bit of flotsam
from the wreckage of your soul, a letter home
returned to sender

a poem says: aw shucks, ma.
its just a scratch. a poem says:
apocalypse now, mutha-fucka.

a poem is a ransom note, a recipe, a lost balloon,
a desperate cry, a warning, a buoy, a mile marker,
smoke, lots of smoke

a shovel, wings, an aqualung, a space capsule, a time capsule,
a capsule of you'll-never-take-me-alive cyanide,
another hole in the ground

a poem is a mythical beast, and a slayer of beasts,
a poem is what's left

Susan Lilley

neighborhood: Winter Park

---

nominated by (Gianna Russo)

Permission

First you learn that after a certain age
you should no longer suck
your thumb in public. Nor should you
wear yard pants with no shirt
or answer the phone "who is it?"
Later, if becomes clear
you should not beat soda machines
or eat all the peppermint ice cream
or make out on the carpet
until you edges shriek
with burning. Then comes a time

you should not untie the top
of your bathing suit while lying in
the sun. The sun! A star that once lavished
its lovelight upon you. The sun,
that stole your beauty one day and moved on,
like a lover changing the locks
while you're at the grocery store.

There is an age past which you must
not flirt with anyone except babies. Not
bartenders, musicians, nor fellow travelers.
You don't need to ask for directions;
the future is deforested. But now
you can roll down the car windows,
listen to Etta James or Cat Power
as loud as you want, love

without losing the hard
jewel under your ribs.

Your scent is the honey
of loyalty. You can lie on a picnic
blanket with your girlfriends
at an art festival, drink wine from a Solo cup,
command the air to turn
from clear to sapphire.

You may dance in a pool
of shade by a darkening lake
and smoke pot with your oldest friend.
Because finally,
no one is paying any attention
to you.

Originally published in *American Poetry Review* and Susan's book *Venus in Retrograde* (Burrow Press, 2019)

Beautyberry by Katarzyna Dutkowska

Gianna Russo

neighborhood: Tampa

nominated by (David Colodney)

Beautyberry
Callicarpa americana

How I come back to you, Florida girl,
reaching up now from my sandy yard
with your couplets and trios of green spades,
your splayed stems like the start of magic.

In fall, your limbs make a yellow-green sprawl,
each branch wearing garnets in duplicate.
They hang on until the Long Night's Moon.
Then you turn naked and wan.

Bush and not bush, chlorophyll, oxygen,
suddenly you're my very own blood,
child and not child, lolling in her swing,
her laugh flitting up like a goldfinch.

I don't want to walk out of this wonderland—
someday I'll have to.
I'll join the long-gone bobwhites,
the cicadas in your shadow.

Florida girl, as your breath skims the world,
I'll hover a while in the sandspur lawn,
retelling the ways I adore you:
the way no-see-ums love moss
and dark seeds adore the earth.

David Colodney

neighborhood: Boynton Beach

nominated by (Anjanette Delgado)

Letter to Michael Pare After Finding *Streets of Fire* on Hulu

Michael, tell me why life does this. Why I stop to notice
raindrops that plop to the pavement outside the shell of the
old Surf Theater & each drop sounds like a phone call from
my past, faint echoes of the lost voices of FM radio deejays
as their smooth growls fade to static. Of course, I stop to
consider each one, try to configure their story, and mine,
narrator of my own plot. And the old theatre, marquee now
splashing CVS instead of the name of some Hollywood
blockbuster, once hangout now metaphor. On the screen I
can see you when *Eddie and the Cruisers* hit theaters. I was
clueless, wandering like teens do, 19 and stuck in between,
not child, not ripe, an unfolding libertine. When *Streets of
Fire* debuted the next year, I saw it here too, and was sure
you shared my obsessions with Springsteen, Morrison, too,
holding shadows of both in your shaman walk
and Seventeen-approved hair. I guess two years on top are
more than most get. Warhol dished out 15 minutes, not
enough time to find a rerun of *Houston Knights* on
Netflix. Life does this, but I don't know why. Back to 19:
it's a bloody age. That summer a kid who graduated with
me rode his motorcycle into a tree and flung slingshot until
he landed on the hood of a passing car right after we'd
seen *The Philadelphia Experiment*, a different role for you.
We killed a summer here, drifting through the cigarette-
smoke glossed movie screens of Saturday matinees
unraveling Eddie Wilson's mystery before drowning our

futures in convenience store wine. How does anyone die at 19? Speed our Kryptonite, I guess, once invincible turned invisible. Tell me why life does this. Tell me why when *Eddie and the Cruisers II: Eddie Lives!* came out six years later, I'd forgotten you. Your cool side-mouth mumble still punctuated your stone-faced monotone, but Eddie was still running wild in sweaty Jersey nights, and I had a degree and a job and left bloody 19 behind like the silver slow roll of movie-ending credits. Tell me why your filmography is long, but your tally of awards is short. Tell me why life does this. Tell me why the rain seems to fall harder when the plot thickens, each drop a story with narration and action, and tell me why one day the phone stops ringing with offers. Just wondering if you could let me know and w/b/s.

Sally Naylor

neighborhood: Coral Springs

---

nominated by (Deborah Denicola)

Ars Poetica

A good poem never cries out loud
or names itself
but might reverberate -- a bit disheveled,
shining like that beamish boy,
chock full of little asides
and gratitude for ear and syllable:

for the full oomph and tongue dance,
all those little riffs of tintinnabulation,
violin crescendos or the solitary brogue of bagpipe,y
robin's warble, clown's guffaw,
mouthing cockney or maybe Yiddish,

it zigzags through cloud

but above all will never recant,
is stuffed with whispered intimacies,
startled by love, a moment so tender and green no gallery can hold it,
so turbulent and whoosh,
you waited all your life   tick tock

for this this this

you will drown happy in it, that heart, that poem, I mean.

Diana Noble

neighborhood: Coral Springs

nominated by (Sally Naylor)

The Boy

He displays contradiction: a fusion of tears and laughter.
A sun-shower, fragmented in raindrops & flecks of light.

He scatters butterflies yet nurtures
spring flowers. With a shift of the breeze:
here then gone.

He mixes, then molds a spectrum of Play-Doh
melding his tones with precision.
Colors each day: sculpting 100 vermillion
monsters, chameleons, and blue guitars.

A silken parasol, strong yet delicate, imprinted
by weathered days, unfurled, as he parades
his ribs and stretchers, how he
clasps the shaft tightly and shelters from tempests.

When closed, he's a Billy club braced for danger.

A wild mushroom, he sprouts quick as weeds.
Nourished by a forest, blooming in the decay,
he labors to climb up among great oaks and fern.

Spawned in searing heat, a raw gemstone,
cast by the confines of imagination, he leans
into the flames then facets himself anew.

Deborah DeNicola

neighborhood: Margate

---

nominated by (Barbra Nightingale)

And After Armageddon . . .

Everything's waiting to open.
Especially the wings of that beached dragonfly,

the one that lit on the sand, observing the gulls,
the effortless gliding of gulls. Their ease and grace

over ruined dunes. And those pipers, their skinny legs
moving as if motored by batteries. I watch as they march

with staccato footsteps, stalking midges and mayflies
in chinks of light, thrilled— just to have survived.

I wait for the ocean to open its benthic rise,
broken sediment, the sea that levels this twilight.

The gulls pull on the capes of their wings,
they know what liberates the four-chambered

heart and opens its ventricles. What small deliverance
we had is now exposed like a castle's casement,

an old oak door we stepped through at the edge
of the moat— Can't we rejoice as the clouds

open their raiment and radiant salmon colors
the sky, calls us to worship the sun--

despite the gift of night coming on?

Notice the brilliance of stars fastened

to the horizon. When will we stop
interrogating our souls, instead throw them wide,

allow them to leave our bones behind to stencil the sand,
taking only the shadows of our appendages—

allowing this world to dissolve
at the threshold of infinite others?

Originally published in *Vox Populi,* June 27, 2022

Romana Tarlamis

neighborhood: Sunrise

nominated by (Sally Naylor)

Pleased to Meet You

Hi, I am an egg-fruit,
nature's
perfect sous-chef offering.

My skin, thin, my flesh, mellow:
school-bus yellow.

As fingers dig in, the olfactory intrigues.
I may not seem charismatic, but wait-

I am baby-food calming belly-blues,
chestnut puréed noodles, pumpkin breads,
toes-in-slippers,
Christmas puddings and happy endings.
Masticate in silence, appreciate.
Cut me a poem, commemorate.

Originally published in a chapbook by *Poetry Box*

PM Draper

neighborhood: Vero Beach

nominated by (Romana Tarlamis)

Corn Moon

Nocturne's orb of harvest
setting in the western sky--
backdropped by September,
showcased spirit of the morning-night.

The river below, flows blue-quiet.
Dolphins break the surface
near the spoil island, pelicans fly-by.
Channel markers blink
 in the rise of dawn
a whiff of citrus in the breeze.

I bike down the bridge, just as I please,
twenty-five miles an hour
 feels like flying--
and I'm a kid again, on that other bridge
when all I had was time
never knowing
what the Corn Moon did.

Michael R. Howard

neighborhood: Vero Beach

nominated by (PM Draper)

My Dhow

I will take you home, somehow
My Dhow,
And sail you along my genteel coast,
As rare a sight would be indeed,
Bumping, shouldering against The Stream.

I will walk your salt cured decks
Where so many knelt in prayer.
Sand and caulk your weathered planks
And clean the Asian borers
From your ancient hull.

My Dhow, who centuries past
Scoured the coast of Zanzibar,
Will now ply our Golden Isles,
Our Treasure Coast,
Where sunken galleons look up
From watery graves with envy.

What shall I carry below
In your ample holds,
Once, heavy laden with dates, fish
And slaves? You labored with grace,
Slid with silent ease past the Shat al-Arab,
Lateen sails astrain, friend and foe astride.

Together, we'll trade your Persian Gulf for ours,
Our nor'easter for your monsoon.

And your wind will be mine, mine yours,
Freely blown,
Your waters, mine, and mine yours.
Salt, dry on your decks, the same
On your tongue and mine.
We will sail the same night skies,
Measure the same stars,
Lift together the same sun and moon.

And though neither of us have yet seen
The Southern Cross.
We will find it together, somehow
My Dhow.

"My Dhow" won a Bronze in the 2021 Florida Writers Association's Royal Palm Literary Awards. It is published in Michael's book of poetry *The Lightning and the Gale*

Untitled by Daria Nepriakhina

Amanda Leal

neighborhood: Lake Worth

nominated by (Craig Ryan)

Portrait at Seventeen

The first time we kissed, my shirt
came up in the wind like the bell
of a flower, my belly soft and white
as meringue. Not yet touched by anorexia, I glowed
in the sunlight that came down like a sheet
over our bodies, my pink hair that invited bumblebees
to orbit my ear, the hands of my first girlfriend
at the valley of my waist. I could not have loved my self
better: the way I swam in my own skin on a bed
of crabgrass, as I shed my family, forgot
the cadence of shame, islands of freckles
on my shoulders, giving to my body exactly
what my body wanted, the climbing vines
of my hands wandering blindly, my hips that bowed
and sank, curved like blown glass.

Miami at Night by Renzo Del Castillo

Mary Jane Ryals

neighborhood: Tallahassee

nominated by (Michael Trammell)

Florence after Lockdown, 2021
—*for Greg, Jonathan and Michael*

On the bones of my ears I hear chatter
all day and all night, the chatter of Saturday city--
the bust-out from lockdown for months
the echo off Santa Croce piazza of dog bark
of horse clip-clop, of dishes clattering,
church bells clanging, the double-door slam
of palacio entrada. In the alleys song of North
Africans calling to god, that release of pain.

Our neighbors who live here say during Covid
Firenze was so quiet that the foxes and porcupines
walked the abandoned city streets. On Sunday
in the Duomo, the pipe organ blasts bass,
vibrates through us like lions, the priest's voice
a rasping tenor, tender surprise. The solo by the alto
reminds my ears of water and wavy glass
in a beach house at sunrise. Where are you?

Where is your sound when you are thinking?
For me, the purple flowers in pots at Le Vespe
Ristorante sing the soprano of the choir woman--
slow vibrato rising as incense up and up. These old
choir songs take me to Appalachian Americana songs
700 years later, only with guitars and banjos, their major
and minor weaving like Penelope's silk gowns. This
wistful prayer, yes that same release of pain.

Florida's natural sea grass by Sharon L. Green

Michael Trammell

neighborhood: Tallahassee

nominated by (Lenny DellaRocca)

Song of the Grasses

In the grass of the old riverbed
I claim the dance of one million species,

balancing on my hands as a way
to greet the noon bells from the church

where all one billion species live, reinventing
themselves as songs in the grasses.

Here is where I make my rhythms,
within ghosts of rivers, balancing on one

leg because the one trillion species
enter the left heel as the song

in the foot of the bells,
a constant kicking, a way to break

the river clear of the grasses,
the insistent whisper of the one being.

Rhonda J. Nelson

neighborhood: Tampa

nominated by (Silvia Curbelo)

Dorothy Hale In a Madame X Dress
after Frida Kahlo's painting, The Suicide of Dorothy Hale

Six a.m. is a solstice between a woman's seasons
Between her music and a wrecking ball. The longest night
Between traffic and a top story suite. The shortest day

Between centuries and circumstance.
Beauty is an avalanche between work of art and housecoat.
After folly, plummeting, frayed as a hem.

Plain is never a woman's proverb.
Every man's rationale a storm: Better a cardinal than a crow.
What other option? Beauty fades, blood stains.

Windowsill, the equator -- Inside the rubber sole
Grips her to the ground, outside, the dark rope pulling
The stiletto heel releasing footloose into the sky's

Cool embrace on her bare shoulders above the scandalous dress.
The difference between hummingbird and dragonfly.
Between lips and whisper.

She falls like a half-muttered phrase.
Then falls like black fruit from the tallest branch.
Lands heavy as thunder.

Chloe Rodriguez

neighborhood: Tallahassee

nominated by (Virgil Suarez)

Abuelo's Dreams

The wives and women gathered in the kitchen,
the island full of foods from home, a night

of nostalgia. *Fricase de pollo, arroz, platanitos,*
But Cuba was decades away no matter

the distance and the men's cigar smoke lingered
in the kitchen, caressing the food with flirtatious

touch, although the smoke played dominoes
with the men in starched guayaberas

on the veranda, it snuck through the small
gaps in windowsills or through the opening

and closing of the doors, as the wives checked in
on their husbands incessantly. My job was to bring

Abuelos's cafecito y croquetas to our company
but I knew better, I was an arbiter between

two worlds, many moons, and waves away
from one another.   Where the kitchen was talk

of life in *Los Estados*, where my Abuelita and
the wives gossiped about who wore what to church.

While outside the men spoke in loud voices
about *La Revolucion* and plotting the ways Castro

might die, how the regime may one day end,
when they could return to the white beaches of

Varadero or to their medical practices
left to the government or desolate in *Habana*.

I walked slowly with a large silver platter adorned
with small coffee cups painted with horrible yellow

polka dots and dark blue lining, a tray of croquetas
and sliced limes. The cigar smoke mixing

with the aroma of my innocence, *Agua de Violetas*
that I was spritzed in after every bath, like every

Cuban child I had met, another reminder
of home that followed us without consent.

The platter fell from my small, slippery hands inches
from the table. *Café* crashing, *tazas* in smithereens,

the food birds in short flights down to the
terracotta tile. My lips wavered, face and ears

grew hot, and the salt began to flow from my
eyes. My grandfather pulled me onto his lap,

his arthritic fingers bent this way and that.
He smiled, chuckled almost at the scene.

He looked me in the eye: *Life is but an empty dream
and then you die.* A saying he believed he learned

from Longfellow, misusing and mispronouncing
often but this was his attempt to merge the worlds

together; to bring the world in the veranda and stitch
it to that of the kitchen, with his broken English.

I was scolded by my grandmother, in her perfect
dress, her hair curled in all the right directions,

she lectured me: how I had to be a lady, that things
must be done with grace and tact; how I had grown

fat since just this morning. My *abuelo* looked up and said,
Dale suave, Mimi. She glared at him, reminded him

Yo soy la que mando aqui. That night, Cuba didn't
seem so many decades, or stars, or waves away.

Hayden Nielander

neighborhood: Tallahassee

---

nominated by (Chloe Rodriguez)

Show Me Swine Racers

I'm going to fly so far under the radar that I scrape the sidewalk,
slow into a saunter, jab my hands into my pockets to make sure
they're empty, drink somebody's tear like it's rain, do 28 in a 30,
set my soft thoughts free to fly south, whatever is turning my gums
red can keep right on, the night I disappear into
is a sunny two in the afternoon and I haven't left my porch, the blues
—come get me, debt—come get me, I'll ride in your van down
to the crater in the woods where they dig
for fossils and we can settle all this can't get any lower business.

There used to be a Hayden with holes in his roof
so he could see the snowy stars in the eyes of a possum.
His shirt was made of rain and there were gobs of air
in his smile, trousers glassing in the cottonbeams of mothlight.
          No, there was no such Hayden.
I'm thinking of a boy I knew
in the parking lot of the
grocery store we worked at
with park-blue surgery eyes, balancing
a future on a switchblade, he flipped
it into his hand, where it's stayed.

That pharmacy used to be a jail, now they've set jail loose
into the air like a stringless balloon
and from the top of the Ferris wheel
I can see the toddlers riding on the
backs of hogs, holding onto the ears
and this little corner of town
in the carnival shine looks

evil as Texas neon.

The gun in me at least puts everything so plainly,
The convenience store called Hayden won't get robbed tonight.
The IHOP cash register called Hayden is going to keep its tens and twenties.
The dark corner called Hayden doesn't need a streetlamp, just enough
black powder to fill the palm of a hand.

.

Cara Nusinov

neighborhood: Lake Worth Beach

nominated by (Kristin Thurston)

Sunsets Then Now

Winters, we biked through gators, and snakes in the Glades. Everyone
did, we were insane, we were young, fearless, bikinied, and we sang
songs of hope and protest, my hippy hair grazing my derriere, my
two-gallon purple hat, a beacon for boys. We walked barefoot through
the bathrooms at Haulover Beach, through that tunnel to the sand,
shouting hellooooooo, our echo, electric laughter. No one was eaten by
a shark or burned in the fires we lit at night on the sand. No rules, no
regulations. We just did what was right and lived politically tolerant,

mostly kind lives. Now, today, chaos and dictators reign, Fear, Horror,
Germs, Smoke, glide by, creating clouds of sorrow strewn like frosted
crystal dinner plates across this horizon, stacked like freshly washed
dread. The sun sinks, white glass against baby blue, a sky circus:
citrus yellow, pink...it fades down, down, backlit by God. Then a haze
somewhere north, orange-gray smoke puffs float on atmospheric
currents. Cameras click-click. Horizontal whites flash bright neon—
peach, aquas. Venus pops through, Mars, photos turn burnt umber,

indigo blazes scream. It's almost as if the sun wears a veil to stay
hidden now that no one shouts joy or plays Frisbee, faceplanting in the
sand. Bitten by heat and fear, all sorts of mayhem appears. Tonight, a
clear evening, this is a place to be...out in the night. Fireflies spit light,
moths flutter in our cellphone lens and dive to nowhere. The moon
hangs...there...palms silhouette, and night herons call to their mates.
Do sunsets and nature endure through slayings, madness and murk?

We stare at ghosts.

Untitled by Gemma Evans

Helen Pruitt Wallace

neighborhood: St. Petersburg

nominated by (Gianna Russo)

To Imagine Hunger

any kind, of which we knew little,
        lucky as we were in our childhood.
Hunger is... a wound, a lost child...

faint smell of a father's cigar—no—
        the red tip of it...sun
snaking through plains, jagged rocks,

or maybe just their scales, that brittle
        lichen lacing up, flaking?
A pause in the angle

of a wrist becomes a white anthurium
        tossed (in a gesture of grief?) there,
by the side of a road.

I remember the ache of that road.
        I watched it for hours back then:
dust kicking up in certain light,

a tinge--of what was it—hunger?
        Did it go by the name of desire?
That mad press of tires, that contact....

Originally published in *Harvard Review*

Lauren Tivey

neighborhood: St. Augustine

nominated by (Carolina Hospital)

Drift Velocity

It was in the afternoons before parents
arrived home from work, that free time
between bus drops and streetlamps
and homework, when we rode Big Wheels

with banana-seat bicycles, multicolored
plastic streamers quivering from our
tufted handlebars, playing cards fastened
to spokes with clothespins, a rhythmic

thwock-thwock-thwock echoing up and down
neighborhood streets, our yells and yawps
bouncing off the faces of split-level homes.
Us savages of suburbia, on the move, liberated,

loosed upon the modest cul-de-sacs of conformity,
the sprinklered lawns of the planet, from backyard
sheds to fetid ponds to broken-glass fields to infinity,
through archipelagos of stars, delinquent constellations,

us space cadets with our skinned knees, hair of twigs,
and Kool-Aid mustaches, we roamed, we roamed,
in the orphan twilight, flung by the winds, by
devious escapades, for the amusement of gods.

And then the call for supper, our mothers' voices
reedy in the dusky air, macaroni and cheese
steaming in avocado kitchens, cartoons squawking
from television consoles, and this is how we lived

our strewn-about days, partially ungoverned
in the anarchy of afternoons, and we pretended
obedience, but our heads were full of interstellar
madness, and our hearts were full of wild grace.

from Lauren's manuscript *Gen X Primer*

Laura McDermott Matheric

neighborhood: Coconut Creek

---

nominated by (Richard Ryal)

Half February

Mrs. Hass, Classroom 1216, 9th Grade Language Arts

St. Valentine's Day clouds
lumbered across my sky,
culled and dispersed. Behind me,
like clear weather, the window gave out:
a dab of red, a dab of gray, white apertures.

Huddled under a desk with students,
I concentrated on something close, something small.
I breathed the breath of eagles, their spirits one with blessings.
I rose and fell in time with the slow river of the Everglades
as it flowed west of my classroom.

Its Sawgrass, the oldest known plant,
a three-dimensional v-shaped stalk with upward-pointing teeth.
To Seminoles and Miccosukee, survival food
when food was scarce.

How could we have known that grace was not scarce
and would eventually fall upon us?

Atrocities in sixteen minutes tucked beneath a desk.
Three deceased in my classroom
begin to sing within my meditation.
The landscape, like God, a circle whose center is everywhere,
whose circumference cannot be defined.
I recall an organ chord,
a soft hymnal during midday cries –

the smell of cordite, acrid and sour.

Apollo Astronauts once described the moon's aroma
like gunpowder.
In the stillness of my classroom,
the small space that pulls me inside, I am out of orbit,
childless by three.
I want to pour myself into the veins of the invisible.
crystalline. Sleep-shaped and sharp,
memory is all mixed up with metaphors.

You can't see the same thing twice.
You cannot unsee what you saw.
A student said he's not sure
if the splatter on him was his or his friend's.

My classroom now a cemetery,
three cypress trees sprouting in the middle
of this grassy water prairie.

Sixteen minutes chiseled into limestone,
the mythic history of Western civilization,
pinpricked through the zodiac.
And these three children rise in the wind
with the other fourteen
eagles gliding over Everglades.

And like these blades of grass,
we survivors have to stand
sharp through drought and storm.

Nothing to dull our teeth.
No one to silence our songs.

Untitled by Blue Hound

Orange Blossom Baby by Kaitlyn Whatley

Liz Robbins

neighborhood: St. Augustine

nominated by (Lauren Tivey)

Wild Sweet Orange

Now in middle age, my haymaking comes
in tiny pouches, often tea, wild sweet orange.
Why do we unequivocally worship youth?
My friends and I say, you couldn't pay me to
go back, as though our teen years (our dewy
skin, our sinewy lines) were a steamy hostel
in a foreign country, a frat party where we
were rarely sober. Hallelujah, here we are,
having clearly—if barely—escaped.
Now the desk lamp flickers like a downtown
club's strobe at midnight, and the purpose
we've always known clarifies: our offspring
will be fine, if we tell them our stories.
If we wait for the tea to brew. We give them
what we carry, bagged and packed, and in
their hands, it turns to tartness and light.

St. Augustine is Florida's first city and our last.

St. Augustine by Lenny DellaRocca

Editor Biographies

Lenny DellaRocca was the co-host of the poetry event, Poetry In A Pub, on the yacht, *Livingstone's Landing*. The yacht was sunk into the New River in Fort Lauderdale. He dubbed the poets who read at the event, *The Boat Poets*. His chapbook *Things I See in the Fire* won the Yellowjacket Chapbook contest. In 2016, DellaRocca started *Interview With A Poet*, which became the online journal, *The South Florida Poetry Journal (SoFloPoJo)*. He was nominated for two Pushcarts and is the curator of this anthology, *Chameleon Chimera: An Anthology of Florida Poets*. He invented the poetry form, Epoem, and is publisher and editor of *Witchery*. He has five poetry collections and is published widely in print and online.

Madison Whatley is a South Florida poet and 2023 graduate of Florida International University's MFA program, where she was the managing editor at Gulf Stream Magazine. Her poetry has appeared in *Variant Literature*, *Cola Literary Review*, *Saw Palm: Florida Literature and Art*, and various other journals. Her manuscript "Hotline Bimbo" was selected as a Semifinalist for the 2023 Berkshire Prize for a First or Second Book of Poetry by Tupelo Press. She is vice president of Purple Ink Press.

Yael Valencia Aldana is an award-winning poet and writer. She is the author of the poetry collection *Black Mestiza* and the chapbook *Alien(s)*. She is a Pushcart Prize winner, and her work has appeared in *Torch Literary Arts*, *Literary Mama*, and *Slag Glass City*, among others. She teaches creative writing in South Florida and is the managing editor of Purple Ink Press. She lives near the ocean with her son and too many pets. You can find her online at YaelAldana.com.

Artists Biographies

Willy Conley, of Hanover, Maryland, is a former biomedical photographer whose photos are featured in the books *Photographic Memories, Plays of Our Own, The World of White Water, Listening Through the Bone, The Deaf Heart, No Walls of Stone, Deaf American Poetry, and Deaf World.* Other publications include: *Drift Travel Magazine, IMAGES Arizona, Saw Palm, American Photographer, Arkansas Review, Baltimore Sun, Carolina Quarterly, Big Muddy, Folio, and 34th Parallel. Conley.* Conley was born profoundly deaf, and is a retired professor emeritus and former chair of theater arts at Gallaudet University (the world's only liberal arts university for deaf and hard-of-hearing students) in Washington, D.C. His ninth book, *Space is deaf like me,* was published *2024.* To see more of his work visit: www.willyconley. com.

Octavia Clarke is a graphic designer and digital artist. For thirty years, she has created works that reflect our humanity with hard digital tools.

Airam Dato-on is a phptgrapher and foodie based in Chicago, Illinois.

Erik Ebright is an Artist, Designer, and Co-Founder of Purple Ink Press. Born in Columbus, Ohio, and graduate from Pratt Institute in Brooklyn. He is currently working on writing books about meditation and transformation while living in Puerto Rico. He has published several books about his travels, as well as coloring books for adults and children. Founder of the now retired co-living community, Casa Del Bodhi, in Little Haiti, Miami, Erik served as a Prayer Chaplain at Unity on the Bay. He later moved to Hawaii, studying pranic healing, and meditation at the Broken Ridge Buddhist Temple.

Renzo Del Castillo is an award-winning and best-selling poet focused on bridging the gaps between people, as well as building connections and empathy through creation, art, integrity, and love. He was born in Lima, Peru, and has spent the last fifteen years as an executive in the healthcare industry. Renzo currently resides in Miami, but he prioritizes traveling to experience and be exposed to the tenets of other cultures. He strongly believes that it is through art that we find the divinity of truth, the pathway of communication with others, and that through this connection, we are made whole.

Lenny DellaRocca was the co-host of the poetry event, Poetry In A Pub, on the yacht, *Livingstone's Landing*. The yacht was sunk into the New River in Fort Lauderdale. He dubbed the poets who read at the event, *The Boat Poets*. His chapbook *Things I See in the Fire* won the Yellowjacket Chapbook contest. In 2016, DellaRocca started *Interview With A Poet*, which became the online journal, *The South Florida Poetry Journal (SoFloPoJo)*. He was nominated for two Pushcarts and is the curator of this anthology, *Chameleon Chimera: An Anthology of Florida Poets*. He invented the poetry form, Epoem, and is publisher and editor of *Witchery*. He has five poetry collections and is published widely in print and online.

Wade Austin Ellis is an Art Director and Photographer based in Florida. Connect with him via Instagram @wadeaustinellis.

Sharon L. Green is an artist, writer, and poet. Her life has become about art and poetry as her language. She has rediscovered her love for all things artistic and is self-taught: sketching, writing poetry, and painting her way through her days. She currently shares her residence between the forgotten coastline in Florida at her beach cottage and her home in a hamlet of Nashville, Tennessee called Leiper's Fork – renowned for their artsy eclectic village. "Given to me is beauty that surrounds, life beholding the verdant green. Bounty in treasures that I can not hold, this life I lead." *Sharon L. Green.*

Alvaro Gutierrez is originally from Colombia. He is an ophthalmologist who is passionate about photography.

Andrew Rader Hanson is a poet and photographer, who lives in South Florida. In his free time, he lifts weights, hikes, spends time by the sea, practices languages, and reads widely. His work has been published by *Spectrum Literary Journal, Pembroke Magazine, The Hong Kong Review* and more. In addition, he was a finalist for the Scotti Merrill Poetry Award. *This Warehouse Manufactures Thirst,* his chapbook, was also published by Bottlecap Press in

2024.

Blue Hound is a passionate photographer who has loved photography since they first manual camera. They enjoy shooting all over the world.

Marquise Kamanke is a photographer and travel influencer.

Iurii Laimin is a photographer who loves nature. Iurii is originally from Russia.

Maria Lysenko is a photographer based in Los Angeles. Contact with her on Instagram @mashathephotographer.

Gina Moriarty is an emerging writer who earned her MFA through Chatham University in Pittsburgh where her thesis was the recipient of the Katherine Ayres Award. She's mostly a nonfiction writer but dabbles in poetry. Typically, her work covers the themes of addiction, heartache, and coincidence beneath an umbrella of hope. Her nonfiction has been published by *Permafrost Magazine, The AROHO Foundation, The Braided Way Magazine, and 3 AM Press.* Her poetry has appeared in *7th-Circle Pyrite, The Brief Wilderness, The Ekphrastic Review,* and *The Classical Poets Society.*

Christina Nwabugo is photographer, director and Researcher based in England. Connect with her on Instagram @bynwabugo

Oladimeji "Oladimeg" Odunsi is a commercial and portrait photographer based in Canada. Oladimeji aims to create striking visual art using original creative approaches and inventions. This approach cuts across both individual and brand collaborations. He is currently a Canon Canada ambassador. and has created works and campaigns for Canon Canada, Foot Locker Canada, MSI, Unsplash, Corby Spirits & wine, Grey Goose Canada, Pixelmator, Godox, ICArt Miami, Pink Squid, Zara Portugal, Andrea Iyamah, Blues Fest, The Creator class, and a host of others. His works of art have also been featured in a Solo exhibition and other art group showcases.

Dillon Pena is a makeup artist and photographer based in Los Angeles.

Ryan Rivas is the author of the text-image book, *Nextdoor in Colonialtown (Autofocus, 2022),* and the novella, *Lizard People (ThirtyWest, 2023).* He is the publisher of Burrow Press and the coordinator of MFA Publishing at Stetson University's Creative writing MFA program. A Macondo Writers Workshop fellow, his work has appeared in *The Believer, The Rumpus, Literary Hub, Necessary Fiction, Queen Mob's Tea House, Best American Nonrequired Reading 2012,* and elsewhere.

Michelle K. Robinson is a fine artist, painter, and photographer. She is based in South Florida but has also worked in New York City and New England. Her goal is to document the beauty of every day.

Jeff Ronci has been a professional artist for some forty years. He sees himself first as a writer and second as a visual artist. Now, his writing plays a supporting role, while his artwork takes now in the spotlight. A lifelong Miamian, he loves capturing images of Florida from his particular perspective and with his particular sensibility.

Sean Sexton was born in Indian River County and grew up on his family's Treasure Hammock Ranch. He divides his time between managing a 700-acre cow-calf and seed stock operation, painting, and writing. He has kept daily sketching and writing journals since 1973. He is the author of three full volumes of poems including *Blood Writing* (Anhinga Press, 2009), *May Darkness Restore* (Press 53, 2019), *and Portals* (Press 53, 2023). He has performed at the National Cowboy Poetry Gathering in Elko, NV, Miami Book Fair International, Other Words Literary Conference in Tampa, FL, and the High Road Poetry and Short Fiction Festival in Winston-Salem, NC.

Cleiton Silva is a nature photographer originally from Brazil.

Robert So is an Autistic photographer, a Myelitis survivor, and a Christian.

Zoe Tribley is an emerging artist who lives in North Florida. The natural world and human to human experiences influence her work, more can be found on Instagram @zoetribleywriter.

Terin Weinberg earned her MFA from Florida International University (FIU) in Miami, Florida. She teaches in the English Departments at DeSales University and Northampton Community College in Pennsylvania. Her work has been previously published and anthologized by journals such as: *The Normal School, Flyway: Journal for Writing & Environment, Split Rock Review,* and more. *When she isn't teaching and writing, Terin is farming with her husband.*

Francesco Ungar is a nature photographer based in Milan, Italy. His goal is to be featured in *National Geographic*.

Katie Whatley is a Queer artist born and raised in South Florida. She is pursuing a minor in fine arts and a bachelor's in political science at Louisiana State University. She resides in Baton Rouge, LA, where she enjoys LSU Tigers football. Her work has been featured in publications such as *805 Lit + Art* and *GulfStream*.

Contributor Biographies

Gabrielle Aboki received her Bachelor of Science in Sales and Marketing from Tuskegee University in 2019 while minoring in English. She graduated from Florida State University with an MFA in Creative writing - Poetry in the Spring of 2023. She currently has publications in *Obsidian Journal and Leavings Literary Magazine*. *Her poetry centers on themes of home, family, matriarchy, memory, and rememory.*

Elisa Albo was born in Havana. Her chapbook *Passage to America* conveys her family's immigrant story, and *Each Day More* is a collection of elegies. Her poems have appeared in numerous journals and anthologies, including *Bomb, Crab Orchard Review, Notre Dame Review, SWWIM Every Day, Two-Countries: Daughters & Sons of Immigrant Parents, and Vinegar* and *Char*. A professor of English and ESL at Broward College, she lives in Fort Lauderdale.

Yael Valencia Aldana is an award-winning poet and writer. She is the author of the poetry collection *Black Mestiza* and the chapbook *Alien(s)*. She is a Pushcart Prize winner, and her work has appeared in *Torch Literary Arts, Literary Mama*, and *Slag Glass City*, among others. She teaches creative writing in South Florida and is the managing editor of Purple Ink Press. She lives near the ocean with her son and too many pets. You can find her online at YaelAldana.com.

Blaise Allen, Ph.D., has published in many journals, including *The American Journal of Poetry, Pink Panther Magazine, The South Florida Poetry Journal, Long Island Literary, Review, Naugatuck, River Review, The Meridian Anthology of Contemporary Poetry, Blue Fifth Review, Long Island Quarterly, and Mothering Magazine*.

Dr. David B. Axelrod was Suffolk County, Long Island's Poet Laureate, and is now Volusia County, Florida, Poet Laureate, and the director of the Creative Happiness Institute in Daytona Beach. Dr. Axelrod has published in hundreds of magazines and anthologies, as well as twenty-four books of poetry, the newest of which is *The Official Rules for Olympic Bed Riding (Bold Venture Press, 2023)*. He is the recipient of three Fulbright Awards including being the first official Fulbright Poet-in-Residence in the People's Republic of China.

Clayre Benzadón is a queer (bi /pan) Sephardic (Mizrahi)-Ashkenazi award-winning poet, educator, foodie, and activist. Her chapbook, *Liminal Zenith,* was published by SurVision Books. Her work has been published in *SWWIM Every Day, Olney Magazine, and Blue Stem Magazine,* among others. You can find her online at clayrebenzadon.com.

Richard Blanco was selected by President Obama as the fifth Presidential Inaugural Poet in U.S. history. More recently, he was awarded the National Humanities Medal from the NEH by President Biden. In 2022, he was appointed the first-ever Poet Laureate of Miami Dade County, where he currently lives in Surfside. Born in Madrid to Cuban exile parents and raised in Miami, cultural identity characterizes his many collections of award-winning poetry, including *Homeland of My Body* (Beacon Press, 2023).

Mary Block lives and writes in her hometown of Miami, Florida. Her poems have appeared or are forthcoming in *Mudfish, Best New Poets 2020, RHINO, Nimrod International Journal*, and *Sonora Review*, among other publications. Her work can be found online at *Rattle, SWWIM Every Day, Aquifer— The Florida Review Online*, and elsewhere. She is a graduate of New York University's Creative writing Program, a 2018 Best of the Net finalist, a 2012 finalist for the Ruth Lilly Poetry Fellowship from the Poetry Foundation, and a Pushcart Prize nominee. Mary is an editor at *SWWIM Every Day*. Her website is maryblock.net.

Chris Bodor is a first-generation American. He was born in Connecticut to an English mother and a Hungarian father. During the past three decades, his poems have appeared in many independent, small, and micro-press publications, such as the *Lummox Journal, Live Nude Poems,* and *New Generation Beats-2022 Anthology*. He served a two-year term as the Florida State Beat Poem Laureate *(2023-2025)*. Bodor is the editor-in-chief of the international literary journal *A.C. PAPA*, which stands for Ancient

City Poets, Authors, Photographers, and Artists. He lives and works in St. Augustine, the Nation's Oldest City.

Steve Bradbury is a Florida-based landscape artist, writer, and translator.

Dustin Brookshire's (he/him) chapbooks include *Never Picked First For Playtime* (Harbor Editions, 2023), *Love Most Of You Too* (Harbor Editions, 2021), and *To The One Who Raped Me* (Sibling Rivalry Press, 2012). He is the co-editor of *Let Me Say This: A Dolly Parton Poetry Anthology* (Madville Publishing, 2023). Visit Dustin online at dustinbrookshire.com.

Gregory Byrd was a Fulbright fellow (Albania, 2011). His poems have appeared in journals such as the *Tampa Review*, *Apalachee Review*, *Cortland Review*, and *Poeteka* (Albania, in translation). Among his poetry books are *Salt and Iron* (Snake Nation, 2014), *At Penuel* (Split Oak, 2011) and *Florida Straits* (Yellowjacket Press, 2005). *The Name for the God Who Speaks* won the Robert Phillips Prize in 2018. He has received a Creative Pinellas Rapid Returns Fellowship, an SPC Distinguished Teaching Award and a Pushcart Prize Nomination. Greg has degrees in writing and literature from Eckerd College, Florida State University and the University of North Carolina at Greensboro. Greg fishes the flats near Clearwater, rides his bicycle and works on his 1966 Ford pickup. He teaches writing and humanities at St. Petersburg College.

Collin Callahan's first collection of poetry, *Thunderbird Inn* (Silver Medal winner in the 2022 Florida Book Awards), is now available from Conduit Books & Ephemera. His poems have appeared in *Granta, Denver Quarterly, Poetry Northwest,* and elsewhere. Collin holds an MFA from the University of Arkansas and a Ph.D. in English and Creative writing from Florida State University in Tallahassee, Florida, where he currently lives and teaches. You can find his work at collincallahanwrites.com.

Rick Campbell is a poet and essayist living in Alligator Point, Florida. His most recent book of poetry is *Fish Streets before Dawn (*Press 53.) Other books include a collection of essays, *Sometimes the Light, Provenance, Gunshot, Peacock, Dog*; *The History of Steel, Setting the World in*

Order, The Traveler's Companion, and *A Day's Work.* His poems and essays have appeared in many journals and anthologies, including *The Georgia Review, Fourth River, Kestrel, Alabama Literary Review,* and *Prairie Schooner.* He's won a Pushcart Prize and a NEA Fellowship in Poetry.

Sarah Carleton writes poetry, edits fiction, plays the banjo, and knits obsessively in Tampa, Florida. Her poems have appeared in numerous publications, including *Nimrod, Tar River Poetry, Cider Press Review, The Wild Word, Valparaiso,* and *New Ohio Review.* Sarah's poems have received nominations for Pushcart and Best of the Net. Her first collection, *Notes from the Girl Cave,* was published in 2020 (Kelsay Books).

Sarah Carey grew up in Tallahassee and has lived in Florida most of her life. A resident of Gainesville for the last 34 years, she is a graduate of the Florida State University Creative writing Program and the author of two poetry chapbooks, including *Accommodations,* winner of the Concrete Wolf Chapbook Award. Her poems have appeared recently or are forthcoming in *Gulf Coast, Sugar House Review, Valparaiso Review* and elsewhere. Her work has been nominated for the Pushcart Prize and the Orison Anthology. Visit her at SarahKCarey.com or on Twitter @SayCarey1.

C.M. Clark's work has appeared in *Painted Bride Quarterly, West Trade Review, Wild Roof Journal, Bookends Review, Prime Number Magazine, Vallum Magazine* (Montreal), *Punt Volat* (Barcelona), and *The South Florida Poetry Journal.* Her work has been anthologized in collections including Anhinga Press's *Rumors, Secrets and Lies, Demeter Press's Travellin' Mama: Mothers, Mothering and Travel, Voices from the Fierce Intangible World* (SoFloPoJo), and *Chasing Light (Yellow Jacket Press).* Clark was a finalist for the Anhinga Press 2021 Chapbook Prize, and runner-up for the Slate Roof Press Elyse Wolf Prize. She also served as the inaugural Poet-in-Residence for the Deering Estate Artists Village in Miami.

David Colodney is a poet living in Boynton Beach, Florida. He is author of the chapbook, *Mimeograph,* and his poetry has appeared in journals including *rust + moth, South Carolina Review, and Door = Jar.* A two-time Pushcart Prize nominee, David holds an MFA from Converse College and an MA from Nova Southeastern University and has written for the *Miami Herald* and the *Tampa Tribune*. He currently serves as an associate editor of *The South Florida Poetry Journal*.

Dorsey Craft is the author of *Plunder* (Bauhan Publishing 2020), winner of the May Sarton NH Poetry Prize. Her work has appeared recently in *Blackbird, Cincinnati Review, Copper Nickel, Poetry Northwest,* and elsewhere. She teaches at the University of North Florida and serves as assistant poetry editor at *Agni*. She is also co-organizer with Jessica Q. Stark of the Dreamboat Poetry Series in Jacksonville, Florida.

Letisia Cruz is a Cuban-American writer and artist. She is the author of *Migrations & Other Exiles* (Lost Horse Press, 2023), selected by Dzvinia Orlowsky as the winner of the 2022 Idaho Prize for Poetry, and *The Lost Girls Book of Divination* (Tolsun Books, 2018). She is the recipient of a 2022 artist grant from the St. Petersburg Arts Alliance and was selected as a 2022 Dali Dozen Emerging Artist for her project *Rituales: An Exploration of Faith in the Caribbean*. Her writing and artwork have appeared in *[PANK], Ninth Letter, The Acentos Review, Gulf Stream, Saw Palm, Third Coast, Duende, Moko, 300 Days of Sun,* and *Black Fox Literary Magazine,* among others. She is a graduate of Fairleigh Dickinson University's MFA program and lives in a witchy cottage on 6th (The Witch On 6th) in Saint Petersburg. Find more of her work at lesinfin.com.

P. Scott Cunningham is the author of *Ya Te Veo (University of Arkansas, 2018), selected by former U.S. Poet Laureate Billy Collins for the Miller Williams Poetry Series. His poems, essays, and translations have appeared in The Nation, American Poetry Review, Gulf Coast, POETRY, A Public Space, Harvard Review, Michigan Quarterly Review, Monocle,* and *The Guardian, among others. A graduate of Wesleyan University, he lives in Miami, FL.* He is the founder of O, Miami.

Silvia Curbelo is the author of two full-length poetry collections, *Falling Landscape and The Secret History of Water,* both from Anhinga Press, and two chapbooks. She has received poetry fellowships from the National Endowment for the Arts, the Florida Division of Cultural Affairs, the Cintas

Foundation and the Writer's Voice, as well as the Jessica Noble Maxwell Memorial Poetry Prize from American Poetry Review. Her poems have been published widely in literary journals and more than three-dozen anthologies and textbooks. A native of Cuba, Silvia has lived in Tampa all her adult life.

Howard Richard Debs is a recipient of the 2015 Anna Davidson Rosenberg Poetry Awards. His essays, fiction, and poetry appear internationally in numerous publications. His book *Gallery: A Collection of Pictures and Words* is a 2017 Best Book Awards and 2018 Book Excellence Awards recipient. His chapbook, *Political*, is the 2021 American Writing Awards winner in poetry. He is co-editor of *New Voices: Contemporary Writers Confronting the Holocaust*, winner of the 2023 International Book Awards for anthologies. He is listed in the Poets & Writers Directory at pw.org/content/howard_debs.

Anjanette Delgado is a Puerto Rican author who has received recognition for her novels *The Heartbreak Pill* (Atria Books, 2009) and *The Clairvoyant of Calle Ocho* (Kensington Books and Penguin Random House, 2014). Her fiction, nonfiction, and poetry have appeared in the *New York Times'* "*Modern Love*" column and opinion sections, *Vogue*, NPR, HBO, *Kenyon Review*, *Prairie Schooner*, *Pleiades Magazine*, CUNY's *Hostos Review*, *The Rumpus*, and *The Boston Review*. As an editor, Anjanette curated the anthology *Home in Florida: Latinx Writers* and the *Literature of Uprootedness* (University of Florida Press, 2021), which earned her a gold medal at the International Latino Book Awards and was recognized as one of three notable anthologies by Poets & Writers in 2021. She holds an MFA in Creative writing from Florida International University and currently resides in Miami, Florida.

Deborah DeNicola's most recent book is *The Impossible (Kelsay Press)*. *Original Human,* was published by Word Tech Communications. She edited the anthology *Orpheus & Company; Contemporary Poems on Greek Mythology,* from The University Press of New England. Previous poetry books include *Where Divinity Begins* (Alice James Books), and three chapbooks. Her memoir, *The Future that Brought Her Here* (Nicholas-Hays/Ibis Press). Among other awards, Deborah has received a National Endowment Fellowship in poetry, The Packingtown Review's Analytical Essay Award in 2008, and the Carol Bly Short Story Award in 2013. Her website is intuitivegateways.com.

Regina Dilgen, Ph.D., served as a professor of English and department chair at Palm Beach State College in Lake Worth, Florida. Her poetry has been published or is forthcoming in the journals *Blueline, Earth's Daughters, Quartler(ly), The Dewdrop, Persimmon Tree, Passager,* and *Apollo's Lute.* Her prose has been published in *Radical Teacher, Teaching English in the Two-Year College,* and in the anthology *The Reality of Breastfeeding: Reflections by Contemporary Women.* She was a featured poet at a Performance Poets of the Palm Beaches reading. She lives in Delray Beach, Florida, where she writes and paints.

Alexa Doran recently completed her Ph.D. in Poetry at Florida State University. Her full-length collection *DM Me, Mother Darling* won the 2020 May Sarton New Hampshire Poetry Prize and was published in April 2021 (Bauhan). She is also the author of the chapbook *Nightsink, Faucet Me a Lullaby* (Bottlecap Press 2019). You can look for work from Doran in recent or upcoming issues of *Pleiades, Witness, Massachusetts Review, pidgeonholes, NELLE,* and *Gigantic Sequins,* among others. For a full list of her publications, awards, and interviews please visit her website at alexadoran.com.

PM Draper is semi-retired and finally finding her inner poet in Vero Beach, FL. Publications include *The Tao of Hibiscus* and a chapbook, *After Pyre.*

Denise Duhamel's most recent books of poetry are *Pink Lady* (Pitt Poetry Series, 2025), *Second Story* (2021) and *Scald* (2017). *Blowout* (2013) was a finalist for the National Book Critics Circle Award. She is a University Distinguished Professor in the MFA program at Florida International University in Miami and lives in Hollywood.

Sara Ries Dziekonski was named Runner-Up in the Press 53 Poetry Award for her manuscript, *Today's Specials,* to be published in the Fall of 2024 as a Tom Lombardo Poetry Selection. Sara is a Buffalo native and holds an MFA in poetry from Chatham University. Her first book, *Come In, We're Open,* which she wrote about growing up in her parents' diner, won the 2009 Stevens Poetry Manuscript Competition. Her chapbooks include *Snow Angels on the Living Room Floor* (Finishing Line Press, 2018) and *Marrying Maracuyá*

(Main Street Rag, 2021), which won the Cathy Smith Bowers Chapbook Competition. Her poems have appeared in U.S. Poet Laureate Ted Kooser's syndicated newspaper column "American Life in Poetry," and in the journals *Slipstream, Potomac Review, SWWIM Every Day, Connecticut River Review,* and *LABOR: Studies in Working-Class History of the Americas,* among others. She is the co-founder of Poetry Midwives Editing and Submission Services and teaches creative writing with Keep St. Pete Lit.

David Eileen is a poet and Ohio native who earned his MFA from Florida Atlantic University while editor-in-chief of the school's literary magazine, *Swamp Ape Review.* They are currently a poetry editor for *Alien Magazine.* Their work has appeared or is forthcoming in *Diagram, Painted Bride Quarterly, Sundress Publication's Best of the Net Anthology, Permafrost,* and *Cherry Tree Review*; many of which can be found at www.eileenwinn.com. Without purple pens, much of their work would not exist.

Abel M. Folgar (b. 1977) is a poet from Caracas, Venezuela of Lebanese and Corsican heritage. He's the co-author of *Odas a Futbolistas (*Hinchas de Poesía Press, 2018, with Yago S. Cura) and translator of Facundo Soto's *Juego de Chicos* (Jitney Books, 2018). His poetry has appeared in *Pidgeonholes, Noble/Gas Qtrly* and *LaFovea.org,* among others. His articles on art, music and food have appeared across the New Times/Village Voice family of publications, *PureHoney Magazine* and numerous digital and print entities since 1999. *Renault 30,* his debut collection of poems, is available from HINCHAS Press, a Los Angeles-based micropress that publishes zines, poetry, poetry in translation, and library science non-fiction.

Oscar Fuentes, aka The Biscayne Poet, is a multidisciplinary artist based in Miami, who has been sharing his talents and love of the arts for more than 30 years. He is the author of nine books of poetry and prose: *Beautiful Women Will Never Know* (2013), *4 Nights With Betsy* (2014), *Vagabond: Selected Poems, Short Stories, and Plays* (2015), *Welcome Home: Poems inspired by 1Hotel South Beach* (2019), *For the Love of Leotards* (2022), and *Honey & Sting: Poems and Short Stories* (2023). Illustrated zine publications include, *Body Furnace* (2021), *The Cock Fight* (2022), *Oscar The Clown* (2022). Oscar drives a 1974 Dodge Dart and uses typewriter tape for a mustache. Connect with him on social media: @thebiscaynepoet.

Tyler Gillespie is an award-winning educator and writer whose work has appeared in the *New Yorker, Rolling Stone, GQ, The Guardian, The Washington Post, Playboy,* and elsewhere. He's the author of the nonfiction collection *The Thing about Florida: Exploring a Misunderstood State* (University Press of Florida, 2021) and two poetry collections *Florida Man: Poems (Red Flag Poetry, 2018)* and the *nature machine!* (Autofocus, 2023). He's a fifth-generation Floridian who currently lives in St. Petersburg. His website is TylerGillespie.com and his Instagram handle is @tyler_gills.

Terry Godbey's poetry collections are *Hold Still, Beauty Lessons, Flame* and *Behind Every Door*. A winner of the Rita Dove Poetry Award, she has published poetry in *Rattle, Poet Lore, CALYX Journal, Florida Review, Apalachee Review, Crab Creek Review* and other literary magazines. She works as a writer at Marriott Vacations Worldwide in Orlando.

Landis Grenville holds an MFA in poetry from the University of Virginia and is currently a Ph.D. candidate at Florida State University. Her work has appeared or is forthcoming in *Michigan Quarterly Review, The Iowa Review, Hanging Loose, Gulf Stream*, and elsewhere. Currently, she lives and teaches in Tallahassee, Florida.

Andrew Rader Hanson lives in Delray, Florida and takes photos, hikes, lifts weights, and reads history and philosophy in his free time. His work has been accepted by *Pembroke Magazine, Midway Journal, Spectrum Literary Journal, and more.* He was also selected as a finalist for the Key West Literary Seminar's Scotti Merril Poetry Award.

Peter Hargitai is the recipient of the Harold Morton Landon Translation Prize from the Academy of American Poets for his translation of *Attila József* in *Perched on Nothing's Branch (1988)*. His poem "Mother's Visit No. 29" was published in Sixty Years of American Poetry with an introduction by Robert Penn Warren and a preface by Richard Wilbur (Abrams, 1996). He is listed in *Harold Bloom's The Western Canon: The Books and School for the Ages.*

Lola Haskins' 14th collection of poetry, *Homelight* (Charlotte Lit Press, 2023), was named Poetry Book of the Year by *Southern Literary Review*. Her previous collection, *Asylum: Improvisations on John Clare* (University of Pittsburgh Press, 2019), was featured in *The New York Times Magazine*.

Michael Hettich's most recent book of poems, *The Mica Mine*, won the Lena Shull Book Award from the North Carolina Poetry Society. A book of new and selected poems was published in 2023 by Press 53.

Michael R. Howard was born in Jacksonville, Florida and returned to his native state after an exciting twenty-six year career as a Naval Officer and Navy SEAL. Florida's eclectic and disparate environment now fuels his imagination and literary efforts. However, at an early age he was inspired by and absorbed the works of adventurous authors such as Robert Louis Stevenson, Jack London, Rudyard Kipling and Alfred, Lord Tennyson. Michael's first book of poetry, *The Lightning and the Gale* was published in 2022. His second book *The Impeded Stream* was published in early 2024.

Holly Iglesias has received fellowships from the National Endowment for the Arts, the North Carolina Arts Council, the Edward Albee Foundation, and the Massachusetts Cultural Council. Her poetry collections are *Souvenirs of Shrunken World, Angles of Approach,* and *Sleeping Things.* She is also the author of a work of literary criticism, *Boxing Inside the Box: Women's Prose Poetry.* Her current project is an annotated collection of letters between her mother and six WWII defense plant co-workers, which eventually led to lifelong friendships.

Judy Ireland is the author of *Cement Shoes,* a poetry collection that won the Sinclair Poetry Prize in 2013. Her poems have appeared in *Hotel Amerika, Calyx, Saranac Review, Eclipse, Cold Mountain, Coe Review, SWWIM Every Day, The South Florida Poetry Journal,* and other journals, as well as in two anthologies, *Best Indie Lit New England, Vol. 2* and *Voices from the Fierce Intangible World.* She is senior poetry editor and reading series producer for *The South Florida Poetry Journal,* co-director of Performance Poets of the Palm Beaches, and teaches at Palm Beach State College.

Yuki Jackson is a Black and Japanese poet and educator. Her poetry has been published in literary journals such as *Four Way Review* and *Cream City Review*, for which she was nominated for a 2021 Best of the Net Award and the 2020 Summer Poetry Prize. Yuki is a regular contributor for the "Poet's Notebook" column of Creative Loafing Tampa Bay and her work has been featured by NPR Next Gen, Spady Cultural Heritage Museum and the Goodwin-Procter law firm. She was also featured as a playwright for The Straz Center's BIPOC Play-Reading Series, showcasing her writing through an interdisciplinary and collaborative performance. For more, her website is YukiJackson.com.

Elizabeth Jacobson's third collection of poems, *There are as Many Songs in the World as Branches of Coral*, will be published by Free Verse Editions, 2024. Her previous full-length collection, *Not into the Blossoms and Not into the Air* won the New Measure Poetry Prize (Free Verse Editions, 2019). She is an Academy of American Poets 2020 Laureate Fellow and a reviews editor for the online magazine *Terrain.org*. "Quantum Foam" was written in Miami Beach, where Elizabeth lived for ten years. She now lives in Lake Worth Beach.

The winner of the 2022 Cider Press Review Book *Award for Inheritance with a High Error Rate (January 2024)*, **Jen Karetnick** is the author of 10 additional poetry collections, including the chapbook *What Forges Us Steel: The Judge Judy Poems* (Alternating Current Press, 2024). Her work has won the Tiferet Writing Contest for Poetry, Split Rock Review Chapbook Competition and more. Jen is co-founder and managing editor of *SWWIM Every Day*. She has recent or forthcoming work in *The American Poetry Review, Bellevue Literary Review* and others. Jen lives in El Portal, Florida. See jkaretnick.com or visit her on Instagram at JenKaretnick or on Twitter at Kavetchnik.

James Kimbrell's poems have appeared in anthologies including the *Best American Poetry* and the *Pushcart Prize Anthology*. The recipient of a Ruth Lilly Fellowship, a Guggenheim Fellowship, and two fellowships from the National Endowment for the Arts, his most recent collection is *Smote* (2015, Sarabande Books). He has taught for over two decades at Florida State University.

Stacie M. Kiner is a former fellow at the Vermont Studio Center and Hannah Kahn Memorial Award recipient. Her poems have appeared in *The Charlotte Poetry Review, Madison Review, Comstock Review, Meridian Anthology of Contemporary Poetry, Apalachee Quarterly, The Ekphrastic Review, Lavender Review*, Panoply, *Rhino*, and *SWWIM Every Day*. Her chapbook, *Inventory,* was published by Finishing Line Press, New Women's Voices Series. Stacie is the former moderator of a poetry talk show in Miami, the essays editor for *The South Florida Poetry Journal* and an urban gardener.

David Kirby *teaches at Florida State University, where he is the Robert O. Lawton Distinguished Professor of English. He has published fifteen poetry collections, including The Temple Gate Called Beautiful* from Alice James Books in 2008. His latest books are a poetry collection, *Help Me, Information,* and a textbook modestly entitled *The Knowledge: Where Poems Come From and How to Write Them.* Kirby is the author of *Little Richard: The Birth of Rock 'n 'Roll,* which the Times Literary Supplement described as "a hymn of praise to the emancipatory power of nonsense" and which was named one of Booklist's Top 10 Black History Non-Fiction Books of 2010. Entertainment Weekly has called Kirby's poetry one of "5 Reasons to Live." In 2016, Kirby received a Lifetime Achievement Award from Florida Humanities, which called him "a literary treasure of our state."

Steve Kronen's collections are *Homage to Mistress Oppenheimer* (Eyewear), *Splendor* (BOA), *and Empirical Evidence* (University of Georgia). His poems have been published or are forthcoming in *Poetry, APR, Salmagundi, The American Scholar, The Southern Review, Plume, The Threepenny Review, Agni, The Paris Review, The South Florida Poetry Journal, Image, Ploughshares, The Yale Review, The Sewanee Review,* and elsewhere. Awards include an NEA, Bread Loaf and Sewanee Writers' Conferences fellowships, the Boatwright Prize from Shenandoah, the Hemley Award from the Poetry Society of America, and three Florida Arts fellowships. He lives with his wife, novelist Ivonne Lamazares in South Miami.

Laurie Kuntz has published two poetry collections *The Moon Over My Mother's House*, (Finishing Line Press) and *Somewhere in the Telling,*

(Mellen Press), and three chapbooks *Talking Me Off The Roof, (Kelsay Books), Simple Gestures, (Texas Review Press), and Women at the Onsen,* (Blue Light Press). *Simple Gestures* won the Texas Review Poetry Chapbook Contest, and *Women at the Onsen* won the Blue Light Press Chapbook Contest. She has been nominated for three Pushcart Prizes and a Best of the Net Prize. She currently resides in Florida, where every day is a political poem waiting to be written. Visit her at: lauriekuntz.myportfolio.com.

Max Lasky is a poet from New Jersey, now residing in Tallahassee, Florida. He is the co-founder and editor-in-chief of the literary magazine *Leavings,* and an assistant poetry editor for *Narrative Magazine.* His poems are published or forthcoming in *American Poetry Review, Painted Bride Quarterly, Frontier Poetry, the Academy of American Poets' 2021 Prize in Memory of Anaïs Nin, The Indianapolis Review, OxMag,* and elsewhere.

Zuleyha Ozturk Lasky is a poet currently living in Tallahassee working towards an MFA in poetry at Florida State University. She is the co-founder and editor-in-chief of *Leavings* and an assistant poetry editor at *Narrative Magazine.* Her poems have appeared in *Adroit, North American Review, Salamander, Nimrod, Palette* and elsewhere. She was selected as a finalist for the 2022 Gregory Djanikian Scholars Prize.

Daniel Lawless is most recently the author of *The Gun My Sister Killed Herself With,* and his book, *I Tell You This Cow,* was released in March 2024. Recent poems appeared in *FIELD, Barrow Street, Prairie Schooner, Ploughshares, Poetry International, Los Angeles Review, upsteet, SOLSTICE, Manhattan Review, Massachusetts Review, JAMA,* and *Dreaming Awake: New Prose Poetry from the U.S., Australia, and the U.K.,* among others. A recipient of a continuing Shifting Foundation grant, he is the founder and editor of *Plume: A Journal of Contemporary Poetry, Plume Editions,* and the annual *Plume Poetry* anthologies.

Amanda Leal is a 30-year-old poet from Lake Worth FL. Her work has been featured or is forthcoming in *CAROUSEL, Tampa Review, White Wall Review, and others.*

Lúcia Leão is a translator and a writer originally from Rio de Janeiro. Her poems have been published in *The South Florida Poetry Journal*, *SWWIM Every Day*, *Gyroscope Review*, *The Blue Mountain Review*, among others. She is a board member of *The Cream Literary Alliance*, a non-profit organization based in West Palm Beach, Florida, and a reviewer for *RHINO Magazine*. She holds a master's degree in Brazilian literature (UERJ, Rio de Janeiro) and a master's degree in print journalism from the University of Miami (Florida).

Susan L. Leary's most recent collection, *Dressing the Bear*, was selected by Kimberly Blaeser to win the 2023 Louise Bogan Award and will be published with Trio House Press in July 2024. She is also the author of *A Buffet Table Fit for Queens* (Small Harbor Publishing, 2023), winner of the Washburn Prize; *Contraband Paradise* (Main Street Rag, 2021); and *This Girl, Your Disciple* (Finishing Line Press, 2019), finalist for *The Heartland Review* Press Chapbook Prize and semi-finalist for the Elyse Wolf Prize. She holds an MFA from the University of Miami.

Mia Leonin is the author of four poetry collections: *Fable of the Pack-Saddle Child* (BkMk Press), *Braid, Unraveling the Bed*, and *Chance Born* (Anhinga Press), and a memoir, *Havana and Other Missing Fathers* (University of Arizona Press). Leonin has published poetry and creative nonfiction in *New Letters*, *Prairie Schooner*, *Guernica*, *Indiana Review*, *Witness*, *North American Review*, and others. She teaches creative writing at the University of Miami in Coral Gables, Florida.

Susan Lilley served four years as Orlando's inaugural Poet Laureate. Her poetry and non-fiction have appeared in *Gulf Coast*, *Poet Lore*, *American Poetry Review*, *The Southern Review*, *Drunken Boat*, *Saw Palm*, *The Florida Review*, *Apalachee Review*, *Sweet*, and other journals. Her two chapbooks are *Night Windows* and *Satellite Beach*. She is a past winner of the Rita Dove Poetry Award and has held a State of Florida Individual Arts Fellowship. She has taught at the University of Central Florida, Rollins College, and Trinity Preparatory School. Her full collection, *Venus in Retrograde*, was published spring of 2019 by Burrow Press. She lives in Winter Park and is a proud native of her beautiful but beleaguered state of Florida.

Jennifer Litt is the author of the chapbook, *Maximum Speed Through Zero* (Blue Lyra Press, 2016) and the full-length poetry collection, *Strictly from Hunger* (Accents Publishing, 2022). Jennifer's work has appeared in several publications, including *Gulf Stream, Jet Fuel Review, Lumina, Naugatuck River Review, NYC Big City Lit, The South Florida Poetry Journal, Stone Canoe, xs Witchery*. She lives in Fort Lauderdale with her cat Tiger Lily where she writes poetry and works as a freelance editor.

Rita Maria Martinez's current poetry raises awareness about triumphs and challenges when navigating life with chronic daily headaches (CDH) and migraines. Her *Jane Eyre*-inspired poetry collection, *The Jane and Bertha in Me* (Kelsay Books), was a finalist for the Andrés Montoya Poetry Prize and a semi-finalist for the Word Works Washington Prize. Rita's poetry appears in publications like *The Best American Poetry Blog, Pleiades, Ploughshares, Wordgathering, West Trestle Review*, and *SWWIM Every Day*. Her poetry was also featured in CLMP's 2023 Disability Pride Month Reading List. The daughter of Cuban immigrants, Rita lives in Miami, Florida, where she tutors neurodivergent students of all ages. She is on Instagram @rita.maria. martinez.poet and X @cubanbronteite, or you can visit comeonhome.org/ ritamartinez.

Laura McDermott Matheric's first book of poetry, *Visions on Alligator Alley,* is an ekphrastic story in verse published by Lominy Books in 2015 inspired by a 2014/2015 residency with Girls' Club Fort Lauderdale. A two-time Endowed Teaching Chair recipient of Broward College and named the 2022 Distinguished Professor by the Association of Florida Colleges, Laura regularly teaches writing workshops and literature courses at Broward College. She was appointed the first Poet Laureate of the City of Coconut Creek in 2022. A native of Broward County, Laura lives in Coconut Creek, Florida, with her husband Walter, and their two daughters Jordan and Lena.

William May first began writing poetry when he was a young boy at a school for learning-disabled students in New York City. Being dyslexic, reading and writing were skills William had to work hard to master, but he believes that the effort and struggle taught him to appreciate language and recognize its power from an early age. William has always had an interest in presenting his works, not only in written formats but through reading and performance. While, in the past, this often took the form of readings in his local community, he is currently focusing on growing his audience through social media posts and his recently launched Podcast, *Argh! Not Another Podcast About Book Publishing*, presenting his poetry in various formats, as well as through his personalized newsletters. A graduate of Sarah Lawrence College and the University of North Carolina's MFA in Creative writing, William currently resides with his fiancée Melissa Myers on the southeast Florida coast. For samples of his work, further information, and links to his social media including Substack, and his podcast, please visit WilliamMayWrites.com.

Maureen McDole is the author of three books of poems, *Exploring My Options* (2006), *Longing for the Deep End* (2011), and *Feast* (2021). She has an English B.A., with a Literary Studies Concentration from the University of South Florida. Her poetry has been set in a variety of different ways including film, dance, spoken word, art installations, Sprechstimme, and traditional vocal works. She hosts a weekly podcast called *The Write Life and has a monthly column in The Artisan Magazine* under the same name, where she is also the literature editor. She is also the host of her literary non-profit Keep St. Pete Lit's weekly podcast *Typewriter Talks*.

Campbell McGrath is the author of twelve books of poetry, most recently *Fever of Unknown Origin* and *Nouns & Verbs: New and Selected Poems*. His work has appeared in scores of literary journals and anthologies, as well as *The New Yorker*, *Atlantic Magazine*, *Harper's* and *The New York Times*. McGrath's writing has been recognized with some of the most prestigious awards in American letters, including a Guggenheim Fellowship, a Witter Bynner Fellowship from the Library of Congress, a United States Artists Fellowship, and a MacArthur Foundation "Genius Award." He lives with his wife in Miami Beach, and teaches in the MFA program at Florida International University.

Becka Mara McKay is a poet and a translator of Hebrew literature. She directs the Creative writing MFA at Florida Atlantic University, where she serves as faculty advisor to *Swamp Ape Review*. Her newest book of poems is *The Little Book of No Consolation* (Barrow Street Press). She lives in Delray

Beach.

Llewellyn McKernan lives in New Smyrna Beach, Florida. She has a master's degree in English (University of Arkansas) and a master's degree in writing (Brown University). She has had six books of poems published for adults and four for children. Her poems have also been published in many journals and fifty-seven anthologies. They have won 107 regional, state, and national awards, and prizes. Her writing mantra is based on a quotation by the French novelist, Colette: "Look long and hard at what gives you the most pleasure, but look even longer and harder at what gives you the most pain."

M.B. McLatchey is a poet and writer living, writing, and teaching in Florida. She is the author of six books, including the award-winning titles *Beginner's Mind* (Regal House), *The Lame God* (Utah State University Press), and *Smiling at the Executioner* (Kelsay Books). M.B. is a Florida Poet Laureate for Volusia County, arts ambassador for the Atlantic Center for the Arts, chancellor for the Florida State Poets Association, poetry reader for a Miami-based journal *SWWIM Every Day,* and professor of humanities at Embry-Riddle University. Her poetry, published both nationally and internationally, has won several awards and fellowships, including the American Poet Prize. Visit her at: www.mbmclatchey.com.

Peter Meinke (Poet Laureate of St. Petersburg, 2009-2015) was the Poet Laureate of Florida. He's published more than 20 books, including eight in the prestigious Pitt Poetry Series, most recently *Lucky Bones (2014). His book, The Piano Tuner,* received the Flannery O'Connor Award for Short Fiction. His latest publication (2015) is a children's book, *The Elf Poem, illustrated by his wife, artist Jeanne Clark.*

Jesse Millner's poems and prose have appeared most recently in the *Grist and Book of Matches.* His work was included in *The Best American Poetry 2013* and *Best Small Fictions 2020.* His latest poetry book, *Memory's Blue Sedan,* was released in March 2020 by Hysterical Books of Tallahassee, Florida. Jesse teaches writing courses at Florida Gulf Coast University and lives in Estero, Florida, with his dog, Lucy.

Caridad Moro-Gronlier is the Poet Laureate of Miami-Dade County, the first woman to be named so in county history. She is the author of *Tortillera* (TRP 2021), winner of The TRP Southern Poetry Breakthrough Series: Florida, and the chapbook *Visionware* (Finishing Line Press 2009). She is a contributing editor for *Grabbed: Poets and Writers Respond to Sexual Assault* (Beacon Press, 2020) and associate editor for *SWWIM Every Day* an online daily poetry journal for women identifying poets. Her recent work can be found at *America's Best Poetry Blog, Let Me Say This: A Dolly Parton Poetry Anthology, Poesia De Protesta, Split This Rock, Limp Wrist Magazine,* and others. She resides in Miami, Florida with her family.

Donald Morrill is the author of three volumes of poetry, including *Awaiting Your Impossibilities* (Florida Book Award), from Anhinga Press, and four books of nonfiction, including *The Untouched Minutes* (Riverteeth Nonfiction Prize). His debut novel, *Beaut*, won the Lee Smith Fiction Prize and was published by Blair. He's been the Bedell Visiting Writer in the Nonfiction Program at the University of Iowa and writer-in-residence at the Smith Poetry Center. He is founder of the Low-Residency MFA at the University of Tampa. You can find him online at donaldmorrill.com.

Sally Naylor's latest chapbook ricochets between manifesto, memoir, *Ars Poetica* and the phantasmagoric, doing what art does best: merging chaos with order and sense with nonsense. Poet, counselor and educator, Naylor, a three-legged stool, has published a poetry guide, *First Light*, for neophyte poets and most recently two chapbooks, *Carnival Sun* and *Synapse Flies into Startle: The Orgasm Book* (New Notes Poetry 2022 and The Poetry Box, 2021), as well as English, gifted, peer counseling and mediation curricula. Travel, readings and workshops intrigue her when she isn't preoccupied with various forms of wordsmithery. She writes reviews and reads for *The South Florida Poetry Journal* and interviews for the Miami Book Fair. She also leads advanced poetry workshops. Currently working on a self-help book, *The Schlepp Factor*, and a new poetry book, *Holy Skeptic*. Naylor teaches and plays on Fridays on Zoom. You can find her on writerscatapult.com.

Rhonda J. Nelson's collections include *A Cold Fruit, Mythological* (Red Mare #24, 2022), *Musical Chair* (Anhinga Press. 2004), *Kahlo* (audio collection with Irritable Tribe of Poets, 2004), *The Undertow* (Rattapallax Press, 2001), and more. She is a Florida Fellow in Poetry 2000-2001, winner of Writer's Exchange 2000 (Poets & Writers, Inc. NYC), and Named Creative Loafing Magazine Best Spoken Word Artist 2018. Rhonda also received the Romeo LeMay Award in Poetry in the 2020 issue of *The Odet*. She has work in many literary journals and anthologies, including *Grabbed* from Beacon Press (2020), *The final Anthology* from Yellow Jacket Press, *Chasing Light* (2020), and the *Rumors, Secrets and Lies Anthology* (Anhinga Press 2022).

Hayden Nielander is from the Florida Heartland. He's an MFA candidate at Florida State University and assistant poetry editor for *The Southeast Review*.

Barbra Nightingale's 10th book of poetry is *Spells & Other Ways of Flying* (Kelsay Books, 2021). She has seven chapbooks and three full volumes of poetry with small presses. Over 200 of her poems have appeared in national and international journals and anthologies. She is an associate editor with *The South Florida Poetry Journal,* a semi-retired professor, and lives in Hollywood, Florida, with her two and four-legged menagerie.

Diana Noble lives in Coral Springs. Her background is in film production, photography, and design. A mother and dreamer, she started writing poetry under the unwavering tutelage of Sally Naylor during COVID and found the process challenging, exhilarating, and satisfying- a bit like gardening. She considers herself a student of life and most definitely a student in the art of poetry.

Cara Nusinov is a poet, teacher, collage artist, poetry therapy practitioner, laughter yoga leader, certified art journal teacher, and speaker who has joyfully led workshops for decades at The Poetry Buffet Party, Laughter Yoga clubs, writer's groups, and conferences, presenting original prompts, enabling participants to develop, write and share new work, as well as laugh and meditate at any age. She is the author of *Unrequited Loves and Other French Kisses,* and the artist/editor of the anthology/sculpture, *The Polka Dot Poetry Peacock,* and occasionally submits one of her thousands of poems for publication. Cara, also Grandmama, calls quirky Lake Worth Beach home.

Michael Mackin O'Mara was born in Brooklyn and lives in West Palm Beach, Florida. The submitted poem was written on the ride home after a poetry reading by Lenny DellaRocca at Warehouse 57 in Hollywood thirty or forty years ago.

Sharlyn Page, a life-long poet, grew up as one of six children in the backwaters of Florida. Her quest is the exploration of the nature of reality, where she has made some progress. The author of over 600 works, she has recently published several winning works in various contests and online journals. One poem, "Benediction," was nominated for the Pushcart Prize and published in *Tangled Locks Journal*. She is preparing a new book, *Alight*, which will be forthcoming in 2024. Her website is sharlynpagepoet.com.

Zoraida "Ziggy" Pastor is the daughter of Cuban exiles. While completing her bachelor>s degrees at Florida International University. Her Everglades poems were exhibited in the park at the Ernest F. Coe Visitor Center. She was featured in Z Publishing House's *Florida's Best Emerging Poets two years in a row. Zoraida is the author of Bear Echoes,* a poetry chapbook sponsored by O, Miami and The Knight Foundation. She has several poems published in *Ice on a Hot Stove: A Decade of Converse MFA Poetry,* edited by Rick Mulkey and Denise Duhamel.

Yaddyra Peralta is a Honduran-American poet, essayist, and editor. She has been the recipient of residencies from The Betsy Writer's Room, Jaffe Center for Book Arts at FAU, and O, Miami Poetry Festival's virtual residency, Off-Shore, for poets of the Caribbean and Caribbean diaspora. Her work has appeared or is forthcoming in *BOMB, Grist, Ploughshares, The Florida Review*, and the anthologies *Eight Miami Poets* (Jai Alai Books), *The Breakbeat Poets, Vol. 4: LatiNext* (Haymarket Books) and *Home in Florida: Latinx Writers and the Literature of Uprootedness* (University of Florida Press), among others. Yaddyra is the recipient of the 2023 Marjory Stoneman Douglas Poetry Award and lives in Miami, FL.

Geoffrey Philp, a Silver Musgrave Medal recipient, is the author of *Archipelagos*, a collection of poems about climate change. Philp's poem, "A Prayer for My Children," is featured on *The Poetry Rail, an homage to 12* *writers who shaped Miami culture.* He lives in Miami and is working on a graphic novel about Marcus Garvey, *My Name is Marcus.*

Catherine Esposito Prescott is originally from Long Island, New York, and her poetry collection, *Accidental Garden,* won Gunpowder Press's 2022 Barry Spacks Poetry Prize (selected by Danusha Laméris). She is also the author of two chapbooks, *Maria Sings* (dancing girl press, 2017) and *The Living Ruin* (Finishing Line Press, 2012). Recent work appears or is forthcoming in *EcoTheo Review, Green Mountains Review Online, MER VOX, Mezzo Cammin, NELLE, Northwest Review, Pleiades, Stirring: A Literary Collection, Valparaiso Poetry Review, Verse Daily,* and *West Trestle Review.* Her second full-length collection, *How We Disappear* (formerly titled *We Were Never Here* and *My Sweet Atlantis*), was a finalist for Michigan State University's Wheelbarrow Books Prize, The St. Lawrence Book Award (Black Lawrence Press), and the Texas Review Press Southern Poetry Breakthrough Prize, and a semi-finalist for the Hilary Tham Capitol Collection competition (The Word Works). Prescott earned an MFA in Creative writing—Poetry from New York University.

Liz Robbins' poetry collection *Night Swimming* won the 2023 Cold Mountain Press Book Contest. Her collaborative chapbook on mental health, Fire Carousel, is newly out from Main Street Rag Press. Her other collections are *Freaked* (Elixir P), *Play Button* (Cider Press Review Press), *Hope, As the World Is a Scorpion Fish* (The University of Nebraska Press), and *Girls Turned Like Dials* (YellowJacket Press).

Chloe Rodriguez is a poet, writer, translator, and a South Florida Native. Chloe has a BA in English with a concentration in creative writing and a minor in philosophy from Florida International University. She is currently an MFA candidate for creative writing with a focus in poetry at Florida State University, where she also teaches English composition. She has poems in the *Delta Review* and *Wingless Dreamer.* Her other works have appeared in *The Windward Review, Poet's Choice,* and elsewhere. Chloe is currently completing her first full-length book of poetry, as well as a memoir. She dreams of a swamp hermitage in the Everglades.

Jonathan Rose is an editor, educator, immigration lawyer, internationally published poet, judge of local, national, and international contests, translator, and arts activist. He has earned the Shining Star Award (from the Arts & Business Council of Miami), which serves "to honor an individual who has been a mobilizing, resourceful and innovative leader, enhancing the quality of life in Greater Miami through the arts."

Laura Sobbott Ross has worked as a teacher and a writing coach for Lake County Schools in Florida and was named Lake County's poet laureate. Her poems have been featured on *Verse Daily and have appeared in Meridian, 32 Poems, Blackbird, Main Street Rag, National Poetry Review*, and elsewhere. She was a finalist for the Art & Letters Poetry Prize and won the Southern Humanities Auburn Witness Poetry Prize. She is the author of two poetry chapbooks and three full-length poetry books. She resides with her husband and granddaughter in Mount Dora, Florida.

Gianna Russo served as the inaugural Wordsmith of the City of Tampa, appointed by Mayor Jane Castor in 2019. She is the author of the poetry collections, *All I See is Your Glinting: 90 Days in the Pandemic*, with photographer Jenny Carey (Madville Publishing, 2022), *One House Down* (Madville Publishing, 2019), and *Moonflower*, winner of a Florida Book Award. She has published poems in *Green Mountains Review, Gulf Stream, Negative Capability*, and others. She is the founding editor of YellowJacket Press, which published chapbooks by over 40 Florida poets from 2006 to 2021. She is an associate professor of English and creative writing at Saint Leo University.

Richard Ryal is a writer and professor with a marketing background. He finds the beauty of this world still outmuscles the gloom, but new lines stalk him whether he's busy or not. His favorite poets push him around, like life itself, and give him a new view. It's like driving around an unfamiliar bend in Northern Arizona.

Mary Jane Ryals hails from the Tallahassee area of North Florida. She's a novelist, short story writer, and poet. At Florida State University she taught professional writing for the business college's Management Department before retiring in 2021. *The Moving Waters* is a collection of her poems. Her latest novel is *Cutting Loose in Paradise*. Additionally, she's an associate editor for the *Apalachee Review*. Mary Jane has frequently taught for FSU in London, Florence, and Valencia, Spain.

Brook J. Sadler is a poet, writer, and professor of philosophy. Her writing can be found in many journals including *Greensboro Review, Missouri Review, Cortland Review, Boiler Journal, Ms. Magazine, CALYX, Kestrel,* and *South Writ Large*. Despite cane toads, hurricanes, alligators, mosquitoes, lightning strikes, theme parks, pythons, rip tides, red tides, and pernicious politicians, she lives and writes in Tampa, Florida.

Ismael Santos is a first-gen Latino poet born, raised, and still living in Miami, Florida, specifically Little Havana/Calle Ocho. She loves Cuban coffee and Walt Whitman.

Jeff Santosuosso is a business consultant and award-winning poet living in Pensacola, FL. His chapbook, *Body of Water,* is available through Clare Songbirds Publishing House. He is editor-in-chief of *panoplyzine.com*, an online journal of poetry and short prose. Jeff's work has been twice nominated for the Pushcart Prize and has appeared in *The Comstock Review, San Pedro River Review, The South Florida Poetry Journal, The Blue Nib, Mojave River Review, The Lake (UK), Red Fez, Texas Poetry Calendar, Avocet, Pif,* and other online and print publications.

Peter Schmitt is the author of six collections of poems, most recently *Goodbye, Apostrophe* (Regal House Publishing). He is a native Miamian. Miami remains his home.

Maureen Seaton has authored two dozen poetry collections, both solo and collaborative. Recent works include *Undersea* (JackLeg) and *Sweet World (CavanKerry),* winner of the 2019 Florida Book Award for poetry. Her honors include the Lambda Literary Awards for both Lesbian Poetry and Lesbian Memoir, the Publishing Triangle's Audre Lorde Award, an NEA, and the Pushcart Prize. She was voted Miami's Best Poet 2020 by The Miami New Times and was professor emerita of English and creative writing at the

University of Miami

Sean Sexton was born in Indian River County and grew up on his family's Treasure Hammock Ranch. He divides his time between managing a 700-acre cow-calf and seed stock operation, painting, and writing. He has kept daily sketching and writing journals since 1973. He is the author of three full volumes of poems including *Blood Writing* (Anhinga Press, 2009), *May Darkness Restore* (Press 53, 2019), and *Portals* (Press 53, 2023). He has performed at the National Cowboy Poetry Gathering in Elko, NV, Miami Book Fair International, Other Words Literary Conference in Tampa, FL, and the High Road Poetry and Short Fiction Festival in Winston-Salem, NC.

Gregg Shapiro is the author of nine books including *Refrain in Light* (Souvenir Spoon Books, 2023). Recent/forthcoming lit-mag publications include *BarBar, Otherwise Engaged Literature and Arts Journal, The Penn Review, Gargoyle, Limp Wrist, Mollyhouse, Impossible Archetype*, and *confetti*, as well as the anthology *Let Me Say This: A Dolly Parton Poetry Anthology* (Madville, 2023). An entertainment journalist whose interviews and reviews run in a variety of regional LGBTQ+ and mainstream publications and websites, Shapiro lives in South Florida with his husband, Rick, and their dog Coco.

Susannah W. Simpson's work has been published in *13th Moon, The Wisconsin Review, The South Florida Poetry Journal, SWWIM Every Day, South Carolina Review, POET, Nimrod International, Poet Lore, Salamander,* and *Xavier Review*, among others. She is the founder and co-director of Performance Poets of the Palm Beaches.

Jessica Q. Stark is the author of *Buffalo Girl* (BOA Editions, 2023), *Savage Pageant* (Birds, LLC, 2020) and four poetry chapbooks, including *INNANET* (The Offending Adam, 2021). She is a poetry editor at *AGNI* and is an assistant professor of creative writing at the University of North Florida. With Dorsey Craft, she co-organizes the Dreamboat Reading Series in Jacksonville, Florida, where she currently resides.

Jim Steele is an Ohio native and author of seven books of poetry who now resides in a small town in Central Florida. Retired from a long career in federal government, he spends his time golfing, writing, and traveling. His eighth book was published in October 2023.

Meryl Stratford's chapbook, *The Magician's Daughter*, won the YellowJacket Press Contest for Florida Poets, and her poem, "Why Things Are The Way They Are," won the Modern Myth Match. Her poems have appeared in various journals and anthologies, most recently *Amsterdam Quarterly*. She is a senior poetry editor for *The South Florida Poetry Journal*.

Nicole Tallman is the author of four collections: *Something Kindred, Poems for the People, FERSACE,* and *Julie, or Sylvia*. She serves as Miami's official Poetry Ambassador, editor of *Redacted Books,* and poetry editor for *The South Florida Poetry Journal* and *The Blue Mountain Review*. Find her on social media @natallman and at nicoletallman.com.

Romana Tarlamis was born in Bratislava, Slovakia and has lived in Cana-da and Australia. She currently resides in Sunrise, Florida. Her artistry has been evolving from the moment she sketched her first bouquet of Hydrangea at age seven. In her current art practice, she works with water mediums, collage and writes poetry.

Lauren Tivey is the author of four chapbooks, most recently *Moroccan Holiday*, which was the winner of The Poetry Box Chapbook Prize 2019. Her full-length collection, *Traveler in the Sunset Clouds* (Main Street Rag Publishing Company) was released in 2022. Tivey's work has appeared in *South Florida Poetry Journal, Saw Palm, Connotation Press,* and *Split Lip Magazine,* among dozens of other publications in the U.S. and U.K. She lives in St. Augustine, Florida, where she teaches English and creative writing at Flagler College.

Kris Thurston has been published in *The Nantucket Review* and *Focus: A Journal for Lesbians.* She won Honorable Mention at the Marblehead Arts Festival in 1986. She's had poems included as part of Yom Kippur services at Congregation Beth El in Sudbury Massachusetts and Temple Israel of West Palm Beach. She was invited to read in February 2021 in a joint poetry/

art Zoom reading with Turtle Studios/Poetry Lab. She has been living in Boynton Beach, Florida since 2014.

Michael Trammell's latest novel is *Rad Sick Record*, published by Hysterical Books. He grew up in South Florida and currently lives in the Florida panhandle in Tallahassee. *Our Keen Blue House*, a poetry collection, was published by YellowJacket Press; other work has appeared in *New Letters*, *The Chattahoochee Review, Pleiades,* and *the G.W. Review*. He's a Senior Lecturer at Florida State University and an associate editor for the *Apalachee Review*.

Julie Marie Wade is the author of 16 volumes of poetry, prose, and hybrid forms, including the lyric essay chapbook, *Fugue: An Aural History* (New Michigan Press, 2023) and the lyric essay collection, *Otherwise* (Autumn House Press, 2023), selected by Lia Purpura as the winner of the 2022 Autumn House Nonfiction Book Prize. A winner of the Marie Alexander Poetry Series and the Lambda Literary Award for Lesbian Memoir and a recipient of grants from the Kentucky Arts Council and the Barbara Deming Memorial Fund. Julie has taught in the creative writing program at Florida International University since 2012. She lives with her spouse, Angie Griffin, and their two cats in Dania Beach.

Sidney Wade resides six months in Maine and six months in Gainesville, FL. He has published eight volumes of poetry, the most recent of which is *Deep Gossip: New and Selected Poems* in 2020. She is professor emerita at the University of Florida, where she taught creative writing and translation for 21 years.

Helen Pruitt Wallace's first collection of poems, *Shimming the Glass House*, won the Richard Snyder Prize for Poetry and a Florida Book Award, and her chapbook, *Pink Streets*, was published by Yellow Jacket Press. Curator of the Dali Poetry Series at the Dali Museum, her individual poems have been published in journals and anthologies including *The Literary Review, Harvard Review, Plume,* and *The Slowdown* Podcast. She earned her Ph.D. in English/Creative writing from FSU, and taught poetry and non-fiction at Eckerd College before serving as Poet Laureate of St. Petersburg (2016-2022).

Brendan Walsh has lived in South Korea, Laos, New England, and Hollywood, Florida. He's the author of six poetry collections. His latest, *concussion fragment, i*s the winner of the 2022 Florida Book Award Gold Medal. He is co-host of the *Fat Guy, Jacked Guy* podcast with Stef Rubino.

Susan R. Williamson is a poet and past director of the Palm Beach Poetry Festival. Her poems have appeared in *Beltway Quarterly, Crab Orchard Review, Paterson Literary Review, Poetry Daily, Poetry East, Smartish Pace, StorySouth,* and *The Virginia Quarterly Review* among others. She holds an MFA in Poetry from New England College and a BA in French Language and Literature from the University of Virginia. Her chapbook, *Burning After Dark,* won the Hannah Kahn Poetry Foundation's 25th Anniversary Prize. Williamson lives in Boca Raton, Florida.

Acknowledgments

Richard Blanco: "Looking for the Gulf Motel" from Looking for the Gulf Motel by Richard Blanco, © 2012. Reprinted by permission of the University of Pittsburgh Press.

P. Scott Cunningham: "Qasida of the Pinecone" from Ya Te Veo. Copyright ©2018 by The University of Arkansas Press. Reprinted with the permission of the publisher, www.uapress.com.

Letisia Cruz: "Nothing of Beauty" from Migrations & Other Exiles. Copyright ©2023 by Letisia Cruz. Reprinted with the permission of Lost Horse Press, losthorsepress.org

Lola Haskins: "The Discovery" from Homelight. Copyright ©2023 by Lola Haskins. Reprinted with the permission of Charlotte Lit Press, charlottelit. org

Michael Howard: "My Dhow" from The Lightning and the Gale. Copyright ©2022 by Michael Howard. Reprinted with the permission of La Maison Publishing, Inc.

Susan L. Leary: "Dressing the Bear" from Dressing the Bear. Copyright ©2024 by Susan L. Leary. Reprinted with the permission of Trio House Press, triohousepress.org

Susan Lilley: "Permission" from Venus in Retrograde: Poems. Copyright ©2019 by Susan Lilley. Reprinted with permission from Burrow Press, burrowpress.com

Catherine Esposito Prescott: "6 am" from Accidental Garden: Poems. Copyright ©2023 by Catherine Esposito Prescott. Reprinted with permission from Gunpowder Press, gunpowderpress.com

Maureen Seaton: "Sweet World" from Sweet World: Poems. Copyright

©2019 by Maureen Seaton. Reprinted with the permission of The Permissions Company, LLC on behalf of CavanKerry Press, Ltd., cavankerry.org.

Meryl Stratford: "Her Education" from Malala: Poems for Malala Yousafzai, ©2013. Reprinted with permission from FutureCycle Press, futurecycle.org

Nicole Tallman: "Poem for the Soft Boys" from FERSACE. Copyright ©2023 by Nicole Tallman. Reprinted with permission from ELJ Editions, elj-editions.com

Sidney Wade: "Burrowing Owl" from Bird Book. Bird Book first published by Atelier26 Books, ©2017. Reprinted with permission from Atelier26 Books, LLC, atelier26books.com

Florida Chimera by Octavia Clarke

Richard's Motel by Michelle K. Robinson

A special thank you to the volunteer editors
at Purple Ink Press for their hard work on this project.

Manging Editor: Yael Valencia Aldana
Founding Editor: Erik Ebright
Senior Editor: Madison Whatley
Editor: Alina Lugo
Associate Editor: Bernard Ramos
Associate Editor: Valeria Rodriguez Flores
Associate Editor: Nina Chatel

www.ingramcontent.com/pod-product-compliance
Lightning Source LLC
Chambersburg PA
CBHW051136120626
46547CB00012B/832